PHYSICAL PRINCIPLES IN THE THEORY OF ECONOMIC GROWTH

Physical Principles in the Theory of Economic Growth

VLADIMIR N. POKROVSKI
Professor of Applied Mathematics

Ashgate

Aldershot • Brookfield USA • Singapore • Sydney

HB
241
.P65
1999

Published by
Ashgate Publishing Ltd
Gower House
Croft Road
Aldershot
Hants GU11 3HR
England

Ashgate Publishing Company
Old Post Road
Brookfield
Vermont 05036
USA

Ashgate website: http://www.ashgate.com

British Library Cataloguing in Publication Data
Pokrovski, Vladimir N.
    Physical principles in the theory of economic growth
    1. Production (Economic theory) 2. Economic development
    I. Title
    338.9

Library of Congress Catalog Card Number: 99-73632

ISBN 0 7546 1118 3

Printed and bound by Athenaeum Press, Ltd.,
Gateshead, Tyne & Wear.

Contents

List of Figures

Preface

From the naive point of view of a physicist, *a production process* suggests some work on transformation of raw materials into semi-finished goods and ready commodities, semi-finished goods into other commodities and so on, work which creates *useful for human being order* in our environment. Modern *technologies* determine that the work can be done by labourers and by some equipment which uses external sources of energy. It is impossible to imagine the modern production process without huge *fluxes of external energy*, a phenomenon which attracts attention of many researchers (Mirovski, 1988).

I try to look at the process of production from general point of view, assuming all our environment to be *a thermodynamic system* which, according to Prigogine (1980), is far from the equilibrium state. One can apply notions and tools of modern thermodynamics (Callen, 1960; Reif, 1974) to describe processes in this system, in particular, the process of production of useful things which ought to be considered as dissipative structures as well as all biological organisms and all artificial things. We know that fluxes of matter and energy are needed to create and maintain such structures (Morowitz, 1968; Nicolis and Prigogine, 1977). Thermodynamic laws are quite general and are applicable to any system, no matter how big and complicated it is. It can be a car, or a building, or production equipment, or the surface layer of the Earth. These laws do not require us to know the structure of the system in all details.

From the point of view of economics, the process of production creates *value* which appears at the first touch of the raw materials by the hand of human being, moves together with its material shape, transfers into other shapes, and disappears at final consumption. One can say that economists investigate processes of origin, movement, and disappearing of value, being hardly interested in its material carriers.

Is it possible to link this point of view with physical understanding of the world? One would be surprised, if it were not. I intend to show that *an objective utility function* as a function of the state of the system can be introduced. It appears to be a measure of order in the environment, that is *negoentropy* of the system. Formulation leads to a unified picture that enables us to relate aspects of our observations of economic phenomena to physical principles, as was envisaged by Georgescu-Roegen (1971). The intention is not to reduce economics to physics but to reach a better understanding of the scientific outlook in the framework of Western culture.

The theory of production, which we shall proceed with, is based on the remarkable observations and developments by classical (Smith, 1776; Ricardo, 1817; Say, 1803; Marx, 1867) and neo-classical (Wicksteed, 1894; Marshall, 1920; Cobb and Douglas, 1928; Harrod, 1939; Domar, 1946; Sollow, 1957, 1970) economists.[1] We shall look for *macroeconomic* (physicist might say: phenomenological) models of a production system. It means that we shall not consider separate factories, firms, *etc.* The smallest unit under consideration is a sector which is assumed to produce a specific product. The basis of our development is *linear input-output model* due to Leontief (1936, 1941, 1986) who uses the representation of production system as a set of coupled sectors everyone of them creates its own product. It has appeared to be a quite useful model which is widely applied to description of functioning and development of production sector of economy (Ciaschini, 1993). I suppose that applicability of the linear input-output model to dynamic situations is extended in this work, so as restrictions imposed by production factors (including energy) and evolution of production system itself, that is, technological changes are taken into account. From physical point of view, the main result of technological progress is substitution of human energy by energy from external sources by means of different sophisticated equipment. Technological changes allow us to use extra amounts of energy which is eventually a source of economic growth. Equations of economic growth, which allow

---

[1] I am sorry to say that it was impossible for me to have read all classic authors which I refer to. What I really studied was Marx's *Capital*. I rely on Blaug (1997) when I refer to some other names here and later. His article (Blaug, 1998) is a useful addition to his magnum opus.

one to investigate trajectories of production system in one-sector and many-sector approaches, are formulated in Chapters 7 and 8.

The principal sources upon which I have drawn are indicated at the end of this book. I would in no way pretend that this is anything approaching a complete bibliography. I suppose, now one can count thousands of books, to say nothing of articles in numerous journals, relating to the discussed problems. Everyone can imagine difficulties arising in front of those who decides to tackle with the problem. Though my monograph represents *A New View of Economic Growth* as well as the book by Scott (1989), my monograph differs from the latter and, as far as I am aware, from other books in important respects. My theory is based on the physical principles and using methods which were used and polished at investigating physical phenomena of the nature. To develop the theory for economic system, I had to use some specific principles among which the interpretation of value as useful for humans order in our environment is a key principle (Section 1.2). The initial phase of the theory might be found to be rather formal but the justification for every theory eventually rests on the agreement between deductions made from it and empirical facts, and on the simplicity and consistency of the formalism. I refer to some statistical data for the USA economy to check the theory. The proposed theory can explain many facts of economic growth, especially, the main fact of recent development, that output expansion has outpaced population growth in the 200 years since the industrial revolution. The theory of economic growth explains the exponential growth of *gross domestic product (GDP)*, which is bigger than the growth of labour, and have the means to describe the deviations from the average exponential growth. Nevertheless, the results ought to be considered mainly as methodological ones. I have presented a mathematical apparatus which can be used to analyse the phenomenon of economic growth. The next and necessary steps of investigation can be envisaged as application of the found principles to history of development of national economies.

This work has been launched as author's translation of the book *Energy, Technical Progress, and Economic Growth. Principles of Ecodynamics (Moscow, 1993)* which was issued in Russian. However, some new material was added, the previous material was rearranged, so the monograph has changed essentially and, in fact, turned into a new book. I do not consider the work to be completed, it is better to consider it as a first step of *A Technological Theory of Economic Growth*. However, it would be helpful to discuss the main assumptions of the theory before the further applications have been made. Any comments would be appreciated.

I hope that the book will prove to be useful to graduate students of different specialities who have some background in physics, economics, and mathematics. In fact, the previous Russian version of the book was used by students of *Applied Mathematics* and *Economic Cybernetics* when I was giving lectures on *Methods of Mathematical Modelling* and *Theoretical Economics* in the *Moscow Institute of Economic and Statistics* in 1990 – 95 years. I especially hope that the monograph could be an introductory text to students of *Ecodynamics*, a subject which considers the development of human population and economic system of the society in conjunction with natural phenomena. I have tried to present topics in a self-consistent way that makes the monograph a suitable source for researchers of different specialities who are interested in the problems of development of mankind.

It is a great pleasure to acknowledge my indebtedness to Professor Edward Mallia of University of Malta who has kindly read through the entire original manuscript and made many valuable suggestions both in content and in language. I am indebted to Tom McNabb who has also read the entire manuscript and made many helpful remarks concerning English of the book.

Vladimir N. Pokrovski
Madliena, MALTA
April 1999

Notations and Conventions

A — input-output matrix with components a_i^j ;

B — capital-output matrix with components b_i^j;

C — consumption matrix with components c_i^j;

E — energy consumed in production;

E^j — energy consumed in sector labelled j;

I — gross investment in production system ;

I_j — gross investment of product j;

I^i — gross investment in sector i;

I_j^i — gross investment of product j in sector i;

K — value of production equipment in production system ;

K_j — value of production equipment of kind j in production system;

K^i — value of production equipment in sector i;

K_j^i — value of production equipment of kind j in sector i;

L — labour in production system;

L^i — labour in sector i;

M — amount of circulating money;

N — number of population;

p — price of energy as a production factor;

p_j — price of product j;

Q_j — quantity of product j in natural units;

t — time;

$U(\cdot)$ — objective utility function, welfare function;

$u(\cdot)$ — subjective utility function;

W — value of the national wealth;

W_j — value of the residential wealth of the kind j;

w — price of labour, wage;

X_j — gross output of product j;

Y — final output, gross domestic product;

Y_j — final output of product j;

Z^i — production of value in sector i;

$\beta = \dfrac{\Delta Y}{\Delta L}$ — marginal productivity of labour at $E = const$;

β_i — marginal productivity of labour in sector i;

$\gamma = \dfrac{\Delta Y}{\Delta E}$ — marginal productivity of energy at $L = const$;

γ_i — marginal productivity of energy in sector i;

$\delta = \dfrac{1}{K}\dfrac{dK}{dt}$ — real rate of capital growth;

$\tilde{\delta}$ — potential rate of capital growth;

ε — energy requirement;

$\bar{\varepsilon} = \varepsilon\,\dfrac{K}{E}$ — dimensionless technological variable;

ε^i — energy requirement in sector i;

$\bar{\varepsilon}^i = \varepsilon^i\,\dfrac{K^i}{E^i}$ — dimensionless technological variable;

$\eta = \dfrac{1}{E}\dfrac{dE}{dt}$ — real rate of energy growth;

$\tilde{\eta}$ — potential rate of energy growth;

Θ — index of labour productivity growth;

λ — labour requirement;

$\bar{\lambda} = \lambda\,\dfrac{K}{L}$ — dimensionless technological variable;

λ^i — labour requirement in sector i;

$$\bar{\lambda}^i = \lambda^i \, \frac{K^i}{L^i} \quad - \quad \text{dimensionless technological variable;}$$

$$\mu \quad - \quad \text{rate of capital depreciation;}$$

$$\nu = \frac{1}{L} \frac{dL}{dt} \quad - \quad \text{real rate of labour growth;}$$

$$\tilde{\nu} \quad - \quad \text{potential rate of labour growth;}$$

$$\xi = \frac{\Delta Y}{\Delta K} \quad - \quad \text{marginal productivity of capital;}$$

$$\xi^i = \frac{\Delta Y}{\Delta K^i} \quad - \quad \text{marginal productivity of sectoral capital;}$$

$$\rho \quad - \quad \text{price index.}$$

Latin suffixes take values $1, 2, \ldots, n$ and numerate products and sectors. As a rule, the upper suffix numerates sectors, the lower suffix numerates products. The rule about summation with respect to twice repeated suffixes is used sometimes.

The chapter number and subsequent number of formula in the chapter are shown in references to formulae.

1 Introduction: Growth of Human Population

This Chapter discusses enormous growth of human population during the centuries. It is assumed that the main factor in the rate of population growth is value of residential wealth which increases during the time. Since Palaeolithic times clothing, shelter and fuel have become necessities of life almost as fundamental as food itself. I shall try to look at our environment from a general point of view, considering all our environment to be *a thermodynamic system*, which is in a far-from-equilibrium state. Thermodynamic laws (Callen, 1960; Reif, 1974; Prigogine, 1980) are quite general and are applicable to any system, no matter how big and complicated it is. It can be a car, or a building, or production equipment, or the surface layer of the Earth, while they do not require us to know the structure of the system in all details. The observed growth of human population on the Earth can be explained quantitatively, if quality of the close environment of human beings, that is, residential wealth is taken into account. A mathematical model of the growth is proposed and investigated. A key problem is to understand the laws of production of commodities. In the last Section the production system is considered as an engine of the growth of human population. However, to keep this engine in action, fluxes of energy must move through the system.

1.1 Classic Laws of Growth

The population of human beings have acquired such great abilities to live in any climate zone of the Earth that the numbers are greatly enlarged. The numbers of human beings N on the Earth according to Carr-Saunders (1936), Clark (1968), Durand (1977), and World Population Projection (1992) are collected in Table 1 and shown in Fig. 1. It can be seen that rapid growth occurred at some moments of history commonly regognised as the cultural revolution (about 10^6 years ago), the agricultural revolution (about 10^4 years ago) and the industrial revolution which started in the 17th – 18th centuries.

1

Table 1 Characteristic parameters for human population

	$N,$ 10^6 man	$b-d,$ year^{-1}	$N/\bar{N}$	$\bar{N},$ 10^6 man	$a^* = r/\bar{N},$ man$^{-1} \cdot$ year^{-1}	$W/N,$ \$/man
10^5 B.C.	0.03			0.03	10^{-6}	1
8000 B.C.	10	0.0006	0.978	10.2	2.71×10^{-9}	10
1000 A.D.	280	0.0004	0.986	284	9.75×10^{-9}	20
1650	516	0.003	0.892	579	4.79×10^{-11}	50
1850	1,171	0.007	0.747	1,567	1.77×10^{-11}	100
1900	1,668	0.007	0.747	2,232	1.24×10^{-11}	200
1920	1,968	0.008	0.711	2,767	1.10×10^{-11}	250
1960	3,308	0.019	0.314	10,530	2.63×10^{-12}	2500
1990	5,268	0.0166	0.401	13,146	2.11×10^{-12}	11000
1995	5,721	0.0151	0.454	12,577	2.2×10^{-12}	14000
2000	6,168	0.014	0.495	12,471	2.22×10^{-12}	18000
2010	7,049	0.012	0.567	12,437	2.23×10^{-12}	30000
2020	7,919	0.0105	0.621	12,753	2.17×10^{-12}	50000

The second and third columns give estimates of total population and rate of population growth due to Carr-Saunders (1936), Clark (1968) and Durand (1977). The projections of these quantities for 2000 - 2020 years are taken from World Population Projections (1992).

During the last four thousand years the number of inhabitants increased from 30 millions till almost 5 billions. One can assume that the enormous growth of human population is connected with special features of the population. This properties are specific for human population not for any other biological population inhabiting the Earth.

To describe the change of number of individuals of human population, one can start (Lotka, 1925; Volterra, 1931; Murray, 1989) with a simple balance equation of growth

$$\frac{dN}{dt} = (b-d)N, \qquad (1.1)$$

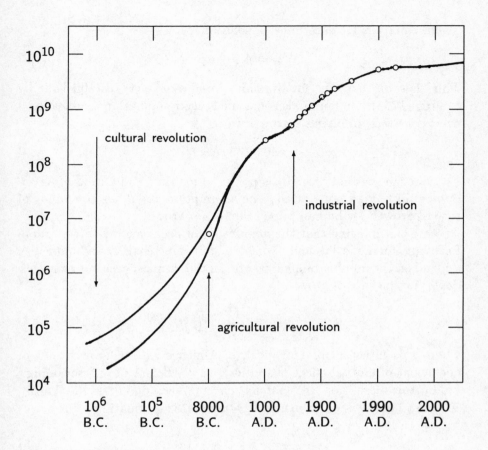

Figure 1 Growth of World population

where b and d are fertility and mortality coefficients, correspondingly.

Equation 1.1 can be applied to any biological population. The form of equation 1.1 is quite general. However, coefficients b and d are determined by circumstances and environment in which individuals of population live. So, these coefficients can depend on the number of species of the same population N and/or some extra variables and we ought to decide what characteristics of environment we have to put into the rate of population growth $b - d$.

In the simplest case, one can assume that rate of growth is constant

$$b - d = r.$$

Then, equation 1.1 determines a solution

$$N(t) = N(0) \exp rt. \tag{1.2}$$

This law of growth for human population was established by Maltus (1798). He found also that unchecked population doubles itself every 25 years, implying a growth rate

$$r \approx 0.0277 \; year^{-1}. \tag{1.3}$$

One can see that this law is not valid for the total period of development of human population. The assumption about the constancy of rate of growth for human population is not true.

One can imagine that the amount of all necessary resources (room for living, food, clothes and so on) are limited, so fertility and mortality depend on the number of inhabitants. In the simplest case one can write down for the rate of growth

$$b - d = r - aN = r\left(1 - \frac{N}{\bar{N}}\right), \quad \bar{N} = \frac{r}{a}, \tag{1.4}$$

where r is intrinsic, or biological, or Malthus rate of growth, a is a coefficient of mutual effect of species or a coefficient of self-poisoning.

In this case, for the population number, one has the known Verhulst (1838) (see, for example, Murray, 1989) equation

$$\frac{dN}{dt} = -a\left(N - \frac{r}{a}\right)N. \tag{1.5}$$

In contrast to equation 1.1 with $b - d = r = const$, equation 1.5 has a steady-state point

$$\bar{N} = \frac{r}{a}$$

which is stable, because $\dfrac{dN}{dt} < 0$ at $N > \bar{N}$ and $\dfrac{dN}{dt} > 0$ at $N < \bar{N}$. So, all trajectories approach asymptotic line $N = \bar{N}$, as it is shown in Fig. 2. Equation 1.5 describes a set of bounded trajectories.

An explicit solution of equation 1.5 can be easily found, if one writes down this equation in the form

$$\frac{dN}{N} - \frac{dN}{N - \bar{N}} = r \; dt.$$

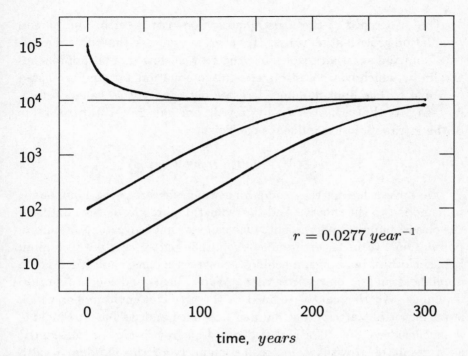

Figure 2 Evolution of population according to equation 1.5

Trajectories approach the line $N = r/a$ from top at $N > r/a$ or from bottom at $N < r/a$. Calculated at $r = 0.0277\ year^{-1}$, $r/a = 10^4$, and different initial values $N(0)$.

Integration of this relation gives a solution

$$N(t) = \frac{\bar{N}\ N(0)\exp\ rt}{\bar{N} - N(0) + N(0)\exp\ rt}.$$

This formula is valid both for $N < \bar{N}$ and $N > \bar{N}$. A graph of solution – the logistic curve – is depicted in Fig. 2. At small times, the population number changes as

$$N(t) = N(0)\left[1 + \left(1 - \frac{N(0)}{\bar{N}}\right)\ rt\right]. \tag{1.6}$$

At big times, in any case, the number has limiting value $\bar{N}$.

One can see that the logistic curve does not describe the human population growth at all times. However, one can see that after the cultural and the agrarian revolutions the growth slowed, as it approaches the limits which can be estimated, due to equation 1.4, and are listed in Table 1. The limit number increases permanently, so value of a decreased. At the earliest stage of growth, one can find a *natural* value of the intrapopulation influence coefficient

$$a \approx 10^{-6} \, man^{-1} \cdot year^{-1}. \tag{1.7}$$

We have a feeling that something which increases the limit ought to be added to the theory. And the 'something' might be the quality of the closest human environment. One can see that individuals of human population live in an environment which is partly created by human being: clothes, buildings, machines, transport means, sanitation, home appliances and so on encircle man. Water, heat, and food come into dwellings. All this can be defined as the artificial environment which is an important attribute of human existence and we have to include it in consideration. The real trajectory of growth can be considered as a result of growth at increasing quantity of the national wealth which decreases the self-poisoning coefficient a or increases asymptotic value of $\bar{N}$.

But which is the measure of artificial environment?

1.2 Artificial Environment and Utility Function

One can note that all artificial things around us have special forms and they are adjustable for using in special aims. In other words, the human being is encircled by a stock of commodities which can be sorted and counted, so that one consider the amounts of quantities in natural units of measurement to be given

$$Q_1, Q_2, ..., Q_n.$$

The forms of artificial things are not occasional. It means that there is some *order* in environment, the order which is created by man and for man. This is special order useful for the human being, so we can call this order U-order shortly.

From the thermodynamic point of view (Callen, 1960; Reif, 1974), negoentropy or negative entropy $-S$ can be a natural characteristic of order (U-order, in this case), while quantities $Q_1, Q_2, ..., Q_n$ can be considered as order parameters, so that one can write down for increase in negoentopy

$$-dS = -\sum_{j=1}^{N} \frac{\partial S}{\partial Q_j} dQ_j, \quad \frac{\partial S}{\partial Q_j} < 0. \tag{1.8}$$

The creation of the order in a system is connected with decreasing of entropy of the system, so that $-S$ is an increasing function of order parameters.

From a different point of view, one can use other characteristics of the stock of commodities, namely, its value. In this case, an empirical estimation of *value of product* is used.[1] The value of unit of product is its *price*. So we assume that the prices of all products are given

$$p_i, \quad i = 1, 2, ..., n.$$

It allows one to estimate increase in value of the stock of commodities

$$dW = \sum_{j=1}^{n} p_j dQ_j. \tag{1.9}$$

It is necessary to take into account that the price of a product is not intrinsic characteristic of the product. The price depends on the quantities of all products which are in existence at the moment. As a rule, the price decreases if the quantity of product increases, though the

---

[1] The concept of value has been introduced when exchanges of different products are considered. 'Therefore, the common substance that manifests itself in the exchange value of commodities, whenever they are exchanged, is their value' (Marx, 1867, p. 14, here and later I cite English translation (1952)). One believes that the products are exchanging according to their values. This is an axiom which gives a relative measure of value, allows one to ascribe certain amount of value to the products and to estimate the value of a set of products. Value is a specific notion of economics, the science which investigates processes of appearing, movement and disappearing of value, being hardly interested in its material carrier. Value is measured in conventional money units (dollar, pound sterling, euro *et cetera*) which are being set when recognised means of circulation (money) is introduced into the economic system (see Section 2.5). History of interpretation of value can be found in work by Blaug (1997) and Gramm (1988).

situation can be more complicated. One can observe that there are coupled sets of products such that increase in the quantity of one product
in a couple is followed by increase (in case of couple of complementary
products) or decrease (in case of couple of substituting products) of the
price of the other product of the couple. So, one ought to consider the
price of a product to be a function of quantities of, generally speaking,
all products

$$p_i = p_i(Q_1, Q_2, ..., Q_n).$$

So as the prices p_i depend on the amounts of products, one can
hardly expect that form 1.9 is a total differential of any function
$W(Q_1, Q_2, ..., Q_n)$. So, one cannot say that W is a characteristics of
the set of the products which is independent of the history. In other
words, the value is not a function of a state of the system. However, a
function of a state which is closely related to value can be introduced.

Indeed, linear form 1.9 can be multiplied by a certain function which
is called integration factor

$$\mu = \mu(Q_1, Q_2, ..., Q_n),$$

so that instead of form 1.9 one has a total differential of a new function

$$dU = \sum_{j=1}^{n} \mu(Q_1, Q_2, ..., Q_n) p_j(Q_1, Q_2, ..., Q_n) dQ_j. \qquad (1.10)$$

Requirements on the integrating multiplier are connected with properties of prices as functions of products, so existence of the function U
depends on the properties of prices. The integrating multiplier can be
taken to be positive, so linear form 1.10 defines monotonically increasing function of each variable. It resembles the behaviour of value. One
can expect that other properties of function U relate to the properties
of value also. In particular, as one expect for the partial derivatives of
value function (if it exists), the ratio of the partial derivatives of the
the function U is equal to the ratio of the prices

$$\frac{\partial U}{\partial Q_i} : \frac{\partial U}{\partial Q_j} = \frac{p_i}{p_j}. \qquad (1.11)$$

Now, to characterise a set of commodities, one has two functions:
$-S$ and U given by their differentials 1.8 and 1.10 correspondingly.

Generally speaking, those are different functions, but they can be connected by a monotonic transformation which does not change the general properties of the functions. So, we can choose the function U to be a characteristic function of the system which describes man-made order in the system – negoentropy connected with artificial things – and utility of this things for human being simultaneously. We can call the introduced function as *utility function (objective)*, taking into account that the properties of function U coincide with those of the conventional *utility function (subjective)* which is used in economics to replace non-existing value function in theoretical consideration.

The traditional way of introduction of utility function as *subjective* utility function is connected with sensation of preference of one aggregate of products as against another (see Section 5.2). The modern analysis of utility was done by von Neumann and Morgenstern (1953), while analogy between theory of utility and theory of heat was stressed in item 3.2.1. Understanding of the fact that utility function U can replace an non-existing value function in theoretical considerations was achieved in the last century (Gossen, 1854; Jevons, 1871; Menger, 1871; Walras, 1874; Marshall, 1920).[2] It was a revolution in economic theory (Blaug, 1997).

So, the important properties of the artificial environment can be characterised by an utility function which, in fact, is a measure of man-made useful order in our close environment or negoentropy of the system. To estimate this quantity, one need to refer to the first law of thermodynamics, according to which

$$
\begin{array}{ccccc}
work & & increase & & flux \\
done & = & in\ internal\ energy & + & of\ heat \\
on\ system & & of\ system & & from\ system.
\end{array}
$$

The last term is connected with change of entropy of the system, that is, $T\,dU$ in our terms, where T is temperature. As far as the change of internal energy of the system can be neglected and the conditions considered to be isothermal, one has proportionality between increase

---

[2] I am sorry to say that it was impossible for me to have read all classic authors which I refer to. What I really studied was Marx's *Capital*. I rely on Blaug (1997) when I refer to some other names here and later.

in utility and total work done on the system, that is,

$$dU \sim dA. \tag{1.12}$$

Increase in value dW is close, but somehow different from change of utility dU, we shall return to discussion of it in Chapter 6. However, proportionality between increase in value dW and total work dA was found at the analysis of empirical data for USA (Costanza, 1980; Cleveland *et al*, 1984). The authors consider these and similar results as confirmation of so-called embodied energy theory of value. However, it is not energy but order which is left in the matter after the work has been done. This order exists and can be, in principle, estimated in an other way. Besides, in contrast to relation 1.12, there is no exact relation between done work and produced value. So, attempts to find embodied energy in artificial things remind attempts to find phlogiston in a body. From all points of view, it is better to regard value as something which is very close to negoentropy of our close environment. Fluxes of products ought to be considered as fluxes of negoentropy not as fluxes of energy.

1.3   Population Growth Affected by Wealth Growth

One ought to assume, that population growth is connected with the economic growth. Interrelation between the two phenomena can be considered from two sides: first, the growth of population determines the extra labour supply in economy and, by this, an option to economic growth at given technology (Barlow, 1994). From the other side, the population growth is determined by the better condition of human existence, that is, eventually, by the results of economic activity which, in its turn, demands labour and other production factors. So, the broader understanding of social and economic development demands more efforts to establish the described interrelation. In this Section, we shall consider the only side of the interrelation, namely, impact of the economic growth on the population growth. The other side will be considered in Chapter 4.

Now, we refer to equation 1.1 for the population number N. Though we do not know all factors affecting the rate of growth $b-d$, we consider value of national wealth W to be of prime importance in the past years of growth of the human population. We shall explore a hypotheses that the rate of population growth $b - d$ in the equation 1.1 is affected by the level of living which, we assume, is described by the value of national wealth per capita W/N. This quantity is being estimated for all countries in our times. For example, it is approximately equal to 40 thousand dollars per man in the USA, but is much lower for most countries of the World. For very ancient time, national wealth per capita W/N can be estimated approximately as value of household consisting of a few animal skins, a primitive dwelling, primitive tools and primitive kitchen appliances in modern prices. Optional estimates of the wealth of the medium inhabitant of the Earth are shown in Table 1. The difference of $10^3 - 10^4$ times between ancient and our times does not seem to be improbable. However, I should like to be corrected at this point.

One can see that the human beings constructs buildings, produces clothes and food, so they lives in the environment which is partially created by themselves. A question can arise; why ought one to take the stock of residential wealth as the main factor influencing on the population growth? Why not the gross national product per capita, or consumed part of GNP per capita? We suppose here that the state of environment rather than the flux of product influences the rate of population growth. Nevertheless, this is a hypotheses which ought to be verified thoroughly. Further on, a mathematical model for the influence of the quantity of the national wealth on the rate growth of the human population is proposed and investigated.

One can start from expression 1.4 for the rate of growth $b - d = r - aN$ in which the self-poisoning coefficient a or the limiting number of population $\bar{N}$ is assumed to depend on the national wealth per capita W/N. The asymptotic value $\bar{N}$ increases, when the national wealth W increases. In the ancient and medieval times, rate of growth of national wealth was very small as compared with the biological rate of growth r, so that population number N was close to the limiting value $\bar{N}$. The ratio $N/\bar{N}$ was close to unity in earlier years of evolution of human population (Table 1), so that deviation of this quantity from unity can be connected with the national wealth per capita

$$\frac{N}{\bar{N}(W/N)} = \left(1 - h\,\frac{W}{N}\right). \tag{1.13}$$

In this formula, h, the coefficient of influence of the national wealth on the rate of population growth is introduced. One can use the previous data and relation 1.13 to obtain a coarse estimates of the influence coefficient

$$h \approx 0.002 \ man \cdot dollar^{-1}.$$

So as the quantity hW/N is estimated to be small for previous years of human evolution, expression 1.13 can be considered as the first two terms of expansion of the ratio with respect to small values of hW/N. To ensure a limiting value of the ratio at bigger values of hW/N, one can generalise formula 1.13 as

$$\frac{N}{\bar{N}(W/N)} = \frac{1 + (s-1)\,hW/N}{1 + s\,hW/N}, \tag{1.14}$$

where the constant s is determined by the asymptotic behaviour of the quantity $\bar{N}(W/N)/N$

$$s = \lim_{(W/N) \to \infty} \frac{\bar{N}(W/N)}{\bar{N}(W/N) - N}.$$

According to formulae 1.4 and 1.14, approximate expression for the rate of growth coefficient takes the form

$$b - d = r \, \frac{hW/N}{1 + s\,hW/N} \tag{1.15}$$

which is equal to zero at $W = 0$ and approaches the ratio r/s at $W \to \infty$.

One can see from equation 1.15 that effect of national wealth is negligible, when

$$h\frac{W}{N} \gg 1.$$

This is the case of the developed countries which have reached the critical amount of national wealth N/h. For them, we have to guess something about asymptotic behaviour of the rate of population growth which is specific and ought to be estimated for every considered nation. So, for example, for the US in recent years on the basis of available data

$$(b - d)_\infty \approx 0.01 \ year^{-1}.$$

However, there are some countries which have not reached the critical value of national wealth N/h. The World population in the whole will have reached the asymptotic behaviour in the next century. So, it is worth applying the description to the growth of population to these countries and to the World.

According to the data of Table 1, the real behaviour of quantity $\bar{N}(W/N)$ for the World in the last decades of our century corresponds to assumption that the quantity has a limiting constant value $\bar{N}^*$, so that one has

$$s = \frac{\bar{N}^*}{\bar{N}^* - N}. \tag{1.16}$$

However, one needs to know real asymptotic behaviour of the rate of growth $(b - d)_\infty$ to determine asymptotic finite values

$$s = \frac{r}{(b - d)_\infty}. \tag{1.17}$$

Formulae 1.15 – 1.17 determine a dependency which obeys to the asymptotic requirements. Of course, there are many expressions which obey these requirements. We choose the simplest one. Taking the above expressions into account, the growth equation 1.1 can be written as follows

$$\frac{dN}{dt} = r \, \frac{hW/N}{1 + s\,hW/N} \, N, \quad s = \min \begin{cases} \dfrac{\bar{N}^*}{\bar{N}^* - N} \\[2mm] \dfrac{r}{(b - d)_\infty} \end{cases}. \tag{1.18}$$

To apply this equation to the growth of human population in recent times and in the future years, one ought to know time dependence of the national wealth W. We can reasonably assume that the rate of national wealth is constant and equal to 0.03 per year in the last decades of our century and in the near future, so that, due to relation 1.16 and using data of Table 1, one can estimate intermediate limiting value of population for the World

$$\bar{N}^* \approx 1.25 \times 10^{10}. \tag{1.19}$$

Then, one can use equation 1.18, to calculate the time dependence of population, whereas asymptotic value of rate of growth $(b - d)_\infty$

is assumed to be no more than 0.01. Population calculated according to equation 1.18 at $r = 0.0277\ year^{-1}$, $h = 0.002\ man \cdot dollar^{-1}$, $\bar{N}^* = 1.25 \times 10^{10}\ man$ and $(b-d)_\infty < 0.01\ year^{-1}$ coincides practically with those shown in the second column of Table 1. The enlargement of W will effect growth of population according to equation 1.5 and gives the curve which is similar to the curve shown in Fig. 1.

The limiting number of population always exceeds its natural (at $W = 0$) value r/a, so that we can write down for number of inhabitants

$$0 < \frac{r}{a} < N < \bar{N}\left(\frac{W}{N}\right) < \bar{N}^*. \tag{1.20}$$

When life support systems are cut off abruptly, i.e., $W = 0$ at $t = 0$ and $N > \bar{N}(W/N)$, one ought to use equation 1.5 which, at small times, according to expression 1.6, determines the law of decrease

$$N = N(0)\left(1 - aN(0)\,t\right), \tag{1.21}$$

where a is a *natural* value of the self-poisoning coefficient.

This is a law of decreasing of population in a case of a World catastrophe. One can apply this law, for example, to the decrease of population in besieged towns.

Thus, one can see that hypothetical dependence 1.15 of the rate of growth on the value of national wealth can qualitatively explain the enormous growth of human population and its decrease when national wealth disappears.

1.4   Energy Principle of Evolution

One can consider the Earth as *a thermodynamic system* which receives fluxes of radiant energy from the Sun and re-radiates heat, whereas a number of transformation is committed with energy on its way through the system (Fig. 3). The Earth and its surface layers are not in equilibrium. Due to the continuing flow of energy from the Sun, they are in a far-from-equilibrium stable thermodinamic state. Due to Prigogine (Nicolis and Prigogine, 1977; Prigogine, 1980), we know that stable dissipative structures can exist in such states. All biological organisms and all artificial things on the Earth can be considered to be dissipative structures which exist due to the fluxes of energy

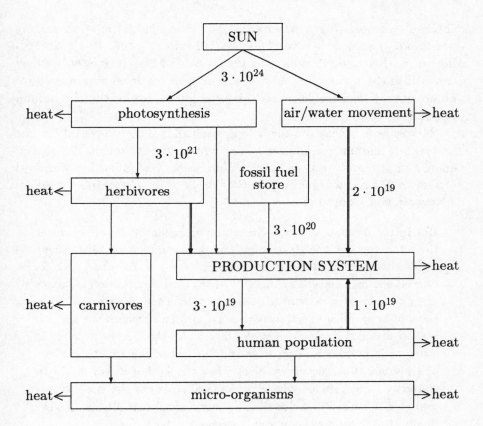

Figure 3 Energy flows in terrestrial systems

The main fluxes of chemical energy (single lines) and mechanical energy (double lines) are shown. Estimates of fluxes (Newman, 1993) in joules per year.

(Morowitz, 1968; Nicolis and Prigogine, 1977). There are dissipative structures of larger scale: convection flows in atmosphere and oceans, ecological systems, socio-economic systems, systems of knowledge and others. However, we only begin to learn to recognise and describe large-scale dissipative structures in the upper layers of the Earth.

Biological population (human population including) is an example of large-scale dissipative structure. The life of every biological population is based on the energy fluxes coming to the population through food and organism of species. One can refer to those fluxes as to *biolog-*

ically organised fluxes of energy. For biological population *energy principle of evolution* is valid (Lotka, 1925; Pechurkin, 1982). According to it, those populations and their associations (ecosystem) which can utilise the greater amount of energy from their environment have an advantage for survival. Can this principle be applied to the human population as well?

It has been suspected for a long time that energy is vital for the survival of human population. The vivid description of the role of energy in the evolution of human population was given by Mumford (1934) in his book, especially in Section 3: *The Elements of Social Energetics* of Chapter 8:

> But in the development of technics the invention of the water-wheel, the water-turbine, the steam engine and gas engine multiplied the energies that were available to man through the use of foods grown for himself and his domestic animals. Without the magnification of human energy made possible through this series of prime movers, our apparatus of production and transport could not have reached the gigantic scale it attained in the nineteenth century. All the further steps in the economic process depend upon the original act of conversion: the level of achievement can never rise higher than the level of energy originally converted, and just as only an insignificant part of the sun's energy available is utilised in conversion, so only a small part of this, in turn, finally is utilised in consumption and creation (p. 376).

According to White (1949), cultural evolution is determined by the control of a progressively greater amount of energy, which is utilised by human societies via improvements in technology.

So, in line with biologically organised fluxes of energy, human population simultaneously has *socially organised fluxes of energy*, while the production system of society plays the role of mechanism attracting the energy from out-of-body sources. The mechanism of utilisation of energy by humans will be considered in subsequent Chapters in more details. Prime sources of energy are the remains of the former biospheres (wood, coal, oil), direct and indirect solar energy (wind, water, tide) and fission and fusion of nuclei. In the middle of the last century the amounts of two fluxes were approximately equal. Nowadays, in developed countries, the socially organised flux exceeds in

$E/N,\ kg\ coal\ equivalent/man \cdot year$

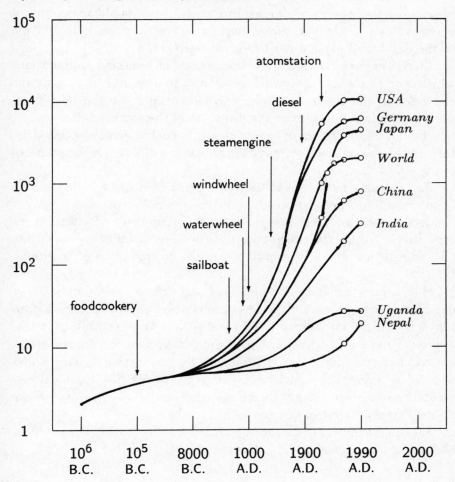

Figure 4   Consumption of energy per capita

Increase in consumption of energy is connected with invention of the more and more sophisticated devices for utilisation of energy sources (wind, runing water, coal, oil, ...). Values for points are taken from Energy Statistics Yearbook (1993 and previous issues).

50 – 100 times the biologically organised flux of energy. Per capita consumption of energy are shown in Fig. 4. Managing huge amount of energy allows the human population to survive in every climate zone of the Earth and expand itself in great measure.

Moreover, one can see from the history of mankind that nations which held available energy had an advantage over other nations. One can refer to the classic example: the industrial revolution and prosperity of Britain began from the invention of the steam engine proper, which allowed utilisation of energy stored in coal in great amount. History of the nations can be rewritten as history of struggle for fluxes of energy.

So, we can conclude that the energy principle of evolution is also valid for human population. The future development of mankind is connected with available energy. Only the abundance of available energy would ensure the prosperous development of human population. Can we get new fluxes of energy or can the consumption of energy be limited?

But, a question is arising here: is it enough to have abundance of available energy to ensure the prosperous development of human population? Georgescu-Roegen (1971) states that another problem could appear. Production of useful things stimulates processes of mixing, dispersion and diffusion, so that necessary for production matter would become progressively unavailable. In other words, the chemical elements become increasingly mixed together and thus more and more difficult to separate from each other.

So, should the Earth be waiting for a diffusion death? The problem is discussed by Ayres (1997b, 1998a).

1.5   Production System

To create and maintain national wealth that is useful for human being things or, in other words, the order in our environment, *a production system* was invented and kept in action. The main constituents of the production system can be seen in Fig. 5. In our imagination, production system is associated with enterprises, factories, plants, and so on which contain a lot of production equipment measured by its value K. The role of production system is to change forms of matter, that is, to

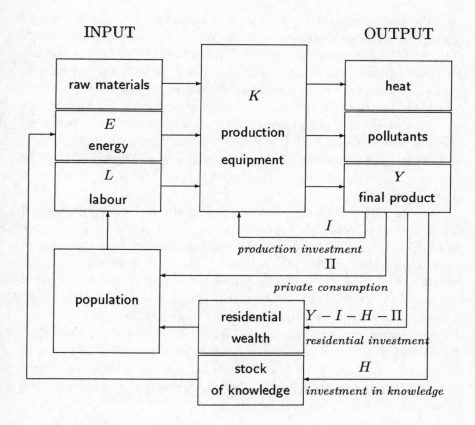

Figure 5 Fluxes in the production-consumption system

transform, for example, ores of different chemical elements into an aircraft which can fly. The result of production process is highly organised matter which is measured by value of final products Y. A part of final product is consumed by human beings, a part goes to enhancement of production system through increase in stock of production equipment. So, the production system itself is a subject to evolution. Of course, it is impossible to avoid emergence of heat and pollutant fluxes, but it is an other side of the problem to which we shall not pay much attention here.

To change forms of matter, work has to be done. The modern *technologies* determine that the work can be done by labourers (labour L)

and by some equipment which uses external sources of energy (energy E). The production system is created for man to live comfortably. At the same time, the man is an element of the production system. The man is built into technological processes, so that the production system is characterised by a number of working places. Then, it is impossible to imagine the modern production process without huge *fluxes of external energy*, phenomena which attracts attention of many researches (Mirovski, 1988). The development of production systems is connected with attracting of a greater amount of external energy. In its turn, attraction of energy appears to be possible due to knowledge of the laws of the nature.

We can refer to Blaug (1997) to follow the fascinating history of approaches the problem of understanding and describing of economic production system. Remarkable observations concerning the process of production were made in frames of classical political economy (Smith, 1776; Ricardo, 1817; Say, 1803; Marx, 1867) and neo-classical economics (Wicksteed, 1894; Marshall, 1920; Cobb and Douglas, 1928; Harrod, 1939, 1948; Domar, 1946, 1947, 1964; Sollow, 1957, 1970).[3] These observations, which are a real basis of the theory of production, allow us to relate some variables to each other. So, according to Smith (1776), Ricardo (1817) and Marx (1867), labour ought to be considered as the only value-creating factor, that is, output can be considered as a function of consumption of labour L

$$Y = Y(L). \qquad (1.22)$$

However, it appeared to be impossible to explain the growth of productivity of labour, that is, the growth of value of commodities produced by unit of labour in unit of time Y/L by use of this simple hypothesis. To explain this empirical fact, other production factors (land and capital) in line with labour were investigated (Wicksteed, 1894). Though once it was told that functional role of machinery in production process was connected with *substitution of labourer's work by work of machines moved by external sources of energy* (Marx, 1867), the amount of production equipment itself (capital K) was taken as important characteristics in a frame of neo-classical economics. So, output Y

---

[3]See the footnote on p. 9.

was written (Cobb and Douglas, 1928) as function of two variables

$$Y = Y(K, L). \tag{1.23}$$

This function is called the neo-classical production function and is used in the theory of production.[4] In relation 1.23 capital K and labour L are regarded as perfect substitutes for one another, that is a given output can be achieved by any combination of the two factors, though of course there is most efficient combination, depending on the prices of production factors. Many particular forms of the function 1.23 are known (Ferguson, 1969).

Since the work of Solow (1957), it is known that the theory based on the neo-classic production function 1.23 does not work properly: technological change appears to be excluded from the theory. Nevertheless, there was a clear understanding that in recent centuries, technological progress was ultimately the source of economic growth in developed countries and it should be incorporated into the theory of economic growth. To avoid the difficulties, a time dependence of function 1.23 (so called exogenous technological progress) was assumed (Solow, 1957)

$$Y = Y(K, L, t). \tag{1.24}$$

A look at recent review papers (Solow, 1994; Grossman and Helpman, 1994; Klenow and Rodriguez-Clare, 1997; Ayres, 1997a, 1998b)

---

[4]Neo-classical tradition relates production of value to quantities of value-created factors, so-called production factors which one needs to create the set of products. The work by Cobb and Douglas (1928) has laid a foundation of a method according to which all factors affecting the production can be considered as arguments of production function. This method has been used up to now. In the last decades, there were some attempts to extend applicability of function 1.23 to reality by including in it new variables such as technology, or human capital, or stock of knowledge H (Grilliches, 1979, 1988; Romer, 1986, 1990; Lucas, 1988), or energy E (Hudson and Jorgenson, 1974; Berndt and Wood, 1979; Kümmel et al, 1985; Kümmel, 1982, 1989). It was assumed that output Y can be written down as a function of three, or more, variables

$$Y = Y(K, L, H, E, ...).$$

It seems there is a belief that the only thing one needs to solve the problem is to find a sufficient number of proper variables. However, having considered the latest developments, Ayres (1997a, p. 32) notes that '...the "right" model specifications is unlikely to be uncovered by econometric analysis of historical data'.

assures us that up to now, despite of investigation of effects of other production factors, the main question about sources of economic growth or, in other words, about the factors of production which can be considered to be sources of the production of value remains.

In this critical situation one ought to look very attentively at the principles of neo-classical theory, especially, at the principle of substitution of labour by capital. One can see that variable K (capital) is playing two distinctively different roles in the neo-classical theory: capital as a measure of value of production equipment and capital as a substitute of labour. There is no doubt that developing of machine technologies appears to give increase in labour productivity. However, the amount of substitution depends not only on amount of production equipment, but also on employed technology. So, perhaps, it would be better to use another independent variable instead of capital in formula 1.23. Although one needs production equipment (capital) to attract extra work of external sources, capital is an intermediate agent to attract energy. Productivity of capital is, in fact, productivity of energy consumed in production.[5] So, we assume that the most natural variable to describe substitution is the amount of energy used in production E which allows us to rewrite function 1.23 as

$$Y = Y(L, E). \tag{1.25}$$

Generally speaking, output is not a function of consumption of production factors at the same moment of time, but a function of trajectory of the past evolution of production factors. We shall came to a more complicated relation 6.18.

It is important to note that introduction of energy as production factor is justified by known results: to maintain order in thermodynamic system, according to thermodynamics (Nicolis and Prigogine, 1977) fluxes of energy are needed to flow through the system. We know (Lotka, 1925; Morowitz, 1968; Pechurkin, 1982) that fluxes of energy are needed to maintain order in biological systems as well. It must be noted that there are now many proponents of the approach to the theory of production from a physical point of view considering

---

[5]Energy, of course, cannot be consumed. I believe that use of the conventional expression *consumption of energy* instead of accurate *work of energy sources* cannot bring misunderstanding.

energy and entropy to be essential variables of description (Allen, 1979; Ayres, 1997a; Cleveland *et al*, 1984; Costanza, 1980; Kümmel, 1982; Kümmel and Linderberger, 1999; Maïsseu and Voss, 1995).

The introduction of energy as a production factor allows us to formulate a theory of economic growth which appears to be a generalisation or re-formulation of the conventional neo-classical approach, so as in addition to neo-classical production factors labour L and capital K, energy E is considered as important variable. Better to say that two roles of variable K (capital) in the previous formulation (capital as a measure of production equipment and capital as a substitute of labour) are separated in our formulation. We consider capital and work to be complements to each other, while energy and labour inputs act as substitutes to each other.[6] Labour and energy are the true sources of value. Capital is the means through which the labour resource is substituted by energy rather than a production factor itself. Scientific and technological progress is incorporated in the pattern of description quite naturally. The main result of technological progress is the substitution of human energy by energy from external sources by means of different sophisticated appliances. The most important characteristics of technology appear to be labour and energy requirements, that is, amounts of labour and energy needed for unit of production equipment to be kept in action. Increasing consumption of energy connected with growth of labour productivity is itself a manifestation of technological progress. However, separate technological variables and equations for them emerge.

The next Chapters contain subsequent derivation of the new theory of production which is the main topic of this book. We use the simplest description when one looks for *macroeconomic* (physicists might say: phenomenological) models of production system. It means that we shall not consider separate factories, firms, *et cetera*. The smallest unit under consideration is a sector which is assumed to produce a specific product. Following Leontief (1941, 1980), one can imagine the production system as a set of coupled sectors every of which cre-

---

[6]Complementarity of energy and capital was analysed by Berndt and Wood (1979). They remark on p. 351 '...that $E - K$ complementarity and $E - L$ substitutability are consistent with the recent high-employment, low-investment recovery path of the U.S. economy.' It means that one cannot consider the variables K, L, E to be independent.

ates its own product. This, so-called *input-output model* is widely used for description of functioning and development of production sector of economy (O'Connor and Henry, 1975; Ciaschini, 1993). In this work, dynamics of production factors (including energy) and evolution of production system itself, that is, technological changes are taken into account.

Result of this consideration can be imagined as equations which connect input variables (labour L, energy E, ...) with output variables (final product Y, national wealth W, ...), namely, equations of economic growth, which allow one to investigate trajectories of development. Equations for production system itself are formulated in Chapter 7 for one-sector system and Chapter 8 for many-sector system. These equations contain exogenous factors: potential rates of growth of labour and energy. Of course, these quantities are endogenous factors in a more complete theory which includes population and stock of knowledge as internal variables. This approach is discussed in Sections 4.4 and 4.5 of Chapter 4. However, very little can be said about 'mechanism of transform of knowledge in energy' at the moment, so that the project cannot be completed in this case.

Through the discussions of the problem, I refer to some data for US economy collected in Appendix to illustrate and to test the theory. I think that it confirms the main assumptions of the theory. However, one ought to consider the results as methodological ones. I have presented a mathematical apparatus which can be used to analyse the phenomena of economic growth. More tests are desirable, and the next and necessary steps of investigation can be envisaged as application of the derived equations to development of national economies.

The description of production system (Fig. 5) from which I have started is conventional. Phenomenological (thermodynamic) approach does not require any important specific assumptions to formulate the theory which contains all elements of neo-classical theory of production and can be considered as generalisation or re-formulation of this theory.

2 Empirical Foundation of Input-Output Model

To describe the action of production system, one has been using basic terms and notions which were introduced by many researchers during a long period of time. Especially important are contributions by Smith (1776), Ricardo (1817), Say (1803), Mill (1840), and Marx (1867) who elaborated the first systems of economic theory (Blaug, 1997). However, definitions of terms are subject to discussion every time one feels that it is time to revise or to demolish old theories to build a new one (Kornai, 1975; Scott, 1989). Though I think that the theory which will be described in the following Chapters is a natural generalisation of neo-classical theory, I follow the tradition and in this Chapter define the sense of the terms one needs to describe the phenomenon of economic growth. The main chain of definitions looks as follows: *product – output – investment – stock of production equipment.* The latter is a set of real means of production: tools and machinery used in production process. I shall use the term *capital* for value of stock of production equipment (means of production). I try to be as close to the conventional usage of terms as possible, so that the available statistical estimates of relevant quantities can be used. In this and following Chapters, for illustration I use time series of some quantities for the USA economy collected in the Appendix.

2.1 On the Classification of Products

The notion of *product* appears to be a fundamental notion of economics. It can be defined as something which is produced to be consumed. It does not matter whether the moment of consumption coincides with the moment of production as, for example, in the case of transport services, or does not. In the latter case the product exists for some time in its material or non-material form. The products are consumed by human beings permanently, so they have to be created permanently. Thus, *a production system* of economy which consists of production units (plants, factories, firms *etc*) exists.

All products, which are created by a production system, can be divided according to aims and modes of their consumption into four groups. First of all, products can be divided with respect to the aim for which they are produced: for *production consumption* or for *final consumption* by human beings. Then, the products can be distinguished with respect to mode of consumption. A product can disappear at consumption at once, as, for example, coal, oil, ore, food and so on. In this case, one talks about *intermediate production consumption* or about *final consumption*. Alternatively, products can be used many times, as, for example, means of production, machinery, means of transport, agricultural land, residential buildings, furniture and so on. In this case one talks about *fixed production capital*, if things are used at production many times, and about *residential wealth*, if products are used as final products many times. Note that sometimes it is difficult to decide whether the product (for example, roads, buildings) ought to be included in production capital or in residential wealth.

Apart from this simple classification, the diversity of products ought to be taken into account. One needs the products to be classified according to any properties to describe internal processes in economy in some details. Nevertheless, one can notice that it is impossible to list all products once and for all. Further on we shall base on assumption that all products can be divided into n classes and shall consider n products to circulate in economy.

We assume, following tradition, that all enterprises of the production system can be divided into n classes as well. So, we imagine that production system of economy consists of n production sectors, each of them produces one product only. In fact, it is not too simple to divide the production system into sectors, nevertheless it appears to be fruitful for the theoretical analysis to divide the production system of economy into production sectors or, more exactly, into *pure production sectors* (Leontief, 1941).

The division of the economy into sectors can be different, the number of sectors depends on the aims one pursues. So, the economy can be divided into no more than a few hundred sectors for current description and planning. A few tens is a good number in this case (see Ciaschini (1993) to find lists of sectors). For research aims, the economy can be divided into a few sectors only (Leontief, 1941, 1986). As an example, one can use a simple model of the production system of an economy consisting of four sectors:

1. Extraction of raw materials (ore, stone, coal, oil, *etc*) for one-time production consumption.

2. Production of means of production and intermediate products: machinery, constructions, transport *etc.* These products can be used one or many times.

3. Creating of principles of organisation: science, research and development, projects and pilot works, education, art, management, computer software. Note that non-material products: principles of organisation, computer software, results of research projects: ought to be related to material production products, as they are useless, unless they are consumed at production. Like material products, they can be consumed once or many times.

4. Production for final one-time and many-times consumption: industry, agriculture, retail trade, restaurants, hotels, construction and maintenance of residential buildings, health care and so on.

The first sector deals with resources for material production.

The second sector produces material production equipment and all material products needed for production. The sector devours the products of the first sector and uses its own products and the products of the third sector in production process.

The third sector produces non-material informational products, which are knowledge and different instructions to human beings on how to organise matter for their use. The instructions are partly realised in the second sector, the other part exists in non-material form as suspended messages, being a great storage of *informational resources* (Gromov, 1985). It is a result of activity of scientific research and project institutes, mainly.

The fourth sector produces the things which the human being needs directly. We can say that we need the first three sectors only to keep the forth sector in action. Human beings do not need the products of the first three sectors directly.

2.2   Movement of Products

We consider an economy to consisting of production sectors, each of them producing its own product. The important characteristic of a sector is its *output*, that is amount of product created by the sector in a unit time

$$dQ_i, \quad i = 1, 2, ..., n.$$

We consider here that these quantities are measured in natural units such as tons, meters, pieces and so on. We do not discuss here the difficulties which appear at essential aggregation of many primary products in the only product of the sector.

To compare the quantities of different products, an empirical estimation of *value of product* is used. The value of unit of product is its *price*. So we assume that the prices of all products are given

$$p_i, \quad i = 1, 2, ..., n.$$

It was discussed in Section 1.2 already, that the price of a product is not an intrinsic characteristic of the product, but is a function of quantities of, generally speaking, all products

$$p_i = p_i(Q_1, Q_2, ..., Q_n). \tag{2.1}$$

We can define *gross output* of a sector i as value of product created by the sector labelled i for unit of time

$$X_i = p_i dQ_i. \tag{2.2}$$

We can consider the gross output of the economy to be a vector with n components

$$X = \left\| \begin{array}{c} X_1 \\ X_2 \\ \cdot \\ \cdot \\ \cdot \\ X_n \end{array} \right\|.$$

To create the product of a sector, apart from fixed production capital, it is necessary to use products of, generally speaking, all the sectors.

For example, to produce bread, it is necessary to have flour, yeast, fuel and so on. So, one can write down for gross output of every sector the balance relation

$$X_i = \sum_{j=1}^{n} X_i^j + Y_i, \qquad (2.3)$$

where X_i^j is an amount of product labelled i used for production of product labelled j. The *intermediate production consumption* of the products is determined by the existing technology. The residue Y_i is called *final output* which will be discussed later.

From the other side, the value of the output of a sector i is a sum of the values of products consumed in production and an additive

$$X^i = \sum_{j=1}^{n} X_j^i + Z^i. \qquad (2.4)$$

This relation defines quantify Z^i which is called *production of value* in sector i. From this point of view, every sector creates value.

The first terms of right-hand sides of relations 2.3 and 2.4 represent products which are swallowed up by acting production sectors. The final outputs of the sectors characterises production achievements of the society. For this purpose, it is convenient to use also the sum

$$Y = \sum_{j=1}^{n} Y_j. \qquad (2.5)$$

This is value of all both material and non-material products created by society per unit of time (year). It is *the gross national product (GNP)* if we consider the national economy.

One can sum relations 2.3 and 2.4 over the suffixes and compare the results to obtain

$$Y = \sum_{j=1}^{n} Z^j. \qquad (2.6)$$

It means that gross national product is equal to the production of value in all production sectors of economy.

The quantities included in formulae 2.3 – 2.6 can be conventionally represented by the following balance table

Gross Output	X^1	X^2	$\cdots$	X^n	Final Output
X_1	X_1^1	X_1^2	$\cdots$	X_1^n	Y_1
X_2	X_2^1	X_2^2	$\cdots$	X_2^n	Y_2
$\cdots$	$\cdots$	$\cdots$	$\cdots$	$\cdots$	$\cdots$
X_n	X_n^1	X_n^2	$\cdots$	X_n^n	Y_n
Production of Value	Z^1	Z^2	$\cdots$	Z^n	Y

All quantities in the table ought to be replaced by numbers if one wants to analyse the real economy.

Gross national product is a measure of current achievements of the economy as a whole. It is a measure of a multitude of fluxes of products. As illustration, gross national product of the US economy measured in constant money scale of value and in current money scale is shown in Fig 6. The upper curve depicts the real change of production of value at constant money scale. In this case the time dependence of GNP can be approximated by exponential functions

$$Y = 1.72 \times 10^{12} \cdot e^{0.0309\,t} \quad dollar(1990)/year. \qquad (2.7)$$

Time t is measured in years, whereas $t = 0$ corresponds to year 1950.

This quantity must be multiplied by *price index* $\rho(t)$ which is a measure of change of money unit of value during the time, to obtain GNP in current money unit

$$\hat{Y} = 19.965 \times 10^9 \cdot e^{0.0518t} \quad dollar/year.$$

Here, time t is measured in years, starting ($t = 0$) from 1900. The real

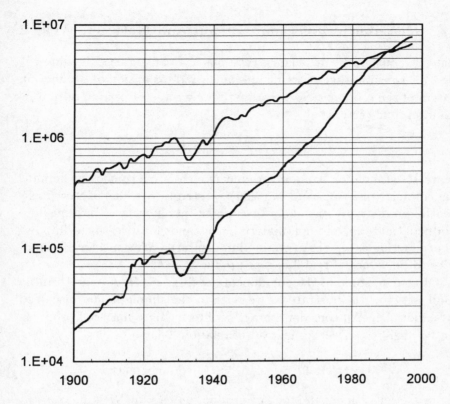

Figure 6 Production of value in the US economy

The steeper curve depicts GNP in millions of current dollars, the other one –
in dollars of year 1990. The latter curve shows real income of the society and
can be approximated by exponential function 2.7.

---

price index is a pulsating quantity, but, from above relation one can
see that the mean price index for the US increases as

$$\rho \sim e^{0.0209\,t}.$$

So, mean value of money unit of the US – dollar – decreases as reversal
quantity. In Section 2.5 we shall return to discussion of price index.

In fact, only the quantity $\hat{Y}$ can directly be estimated for an economy. After some cumbersome procedures (Afriat, 1977), price index
and final output in constant prices can be calculated.

2.3   Distribution of Final Output and National Wealth

The final output Y_j in balance relations 2.3 can be used in different ways for consumption or for maintenance and expansion of production system of the economy. So we can write down vector of final output as a sum of four vectors

$$Y_j = I_j + H_j + J_j + \Pi_j, \qquad (2.8)$$

where Π_j stands for value of product which is consumed by humans immediately (one-time consumption); J_j stands for value of stored residential product; H_j stands for investment into storage of intermediate products (material and non-material); I_j stands for investment into basic production equipment (production capital).[1] We consider all quantities to be values of real fluxes of products.

Of course, some of the components of fluxes I, H, J, and Π can be equal to zero. To illustrate it, we refer to the simple model discussed in Section 2.1. We consider storage of intermediate material products can be neglected here, so, instead of relation 2.8, we have

$$Y_1 = 0, \quad Y_2 = I, \quad Y_3 = H, \quad Y_4 = J + \Pi,$$

where I is investment in stock of production capital, H is investment into stock of knowledge, J is investment in stock of residential wealth, and Π is one-time human consumption. So, one can write down for final output

$$Y = I + H + J + \Pi. \qquad (2.9)$$

The gross investment I_j, H_j, and J_j represent increase of material and non-material wealth per unit of time. We ought to subtract the

---

[1]One of the main question to decide is which are the rules to determine investment into production system. The investment into production equipment determines the development of production system. So, the future production and consumption depend on the today's investment. At any moment of time a society has to decide a problem: what part of the final product ought to be consumed and what part ought to be saved for the sake of future consumption. We can imagine two alternative approaches to the problem: from the side of consumption and from the side of production. In Chapter 4, it is discussed how investment can be determined from the side of production. In Section 7.6 we shall discuss known (Blanchard and Fisher, 1989) models which determines investment at procedure of maximisation of present and future consumption.

value of products, which disappear for the same time (value of depreciation), to obtain *pure investment* into corresponding parts of national wealth

$$\frac{dK_j}{dt} = I_j - \mu K_j, \tag{2.10}$$

$$\frac{dR_j}{dt} = H_j - \mu R_j, \tag{2.11}$$

$$\frac{dW_j}{dt} = J_j - \mu W_j. \tag{2.12}$$

These equations introduce stocks of products: K_j is value of basic production equipment (production capital); R_j is value of storage of intermediate production materials including the stock of knowledge; W_j is value of storage of residential wealth (residential capital). We assume in relations 2.10 – 2.12 that the depreciation is proportional to the amount of national wealth. Generally speaking, coefficients of depreciation are different for different equipment in different sectors. Here and further on for the sake of simplicity, we consider μ to be the same in all situations for all products.

The above relations allow one to represent the components of the national wealth in the following form

$$K_j(t) = \int_0^\infty e^{-\mu x} I_j(t - x)\, dx, \tag{2.13}$$

$$R_j(t) = \int_0^\infty e^{-\mu x} H_j(t - x)\, dx, \tag{2.14}$$

$$W_j(t) = \int_0^\infty e^{-\mu x} J_j(t - x)\, dx. \tag{2.15}$$

We can see that the national wealth is constituted by the investments, especially, by investments of the recent past, or, in other words, capital stock represents accumulative investment. National wealth is a set of commodities: buildings, networks of supply, machinery, transport means, furniture, home appliances and so on. Value of national wealth is a sum of the quantities which were defined above

$$V = \sum_{j=1}^n (K_j + R_j + W_j). \tag{2.16}$$

National wealth consists of products which were produced at different moments of time and under different conditions of production which implies different current prices. Value of national wealth V is a characteristic of the set of the products which dependes of the history of current prices. In other words, value of national wealth is not a point function. However, such a point function for a set of products or a function of a state, which is closely related to value, namely, utility function, can be introduced (see Section 1.2). Utility function U replaces the non-existing value function in theoretical consideration.

Note that relations 2.10 – 2.12 and 2.13 – 2.15 connect with each other two kinds of quantities: fluxes: I_j, H_j, J_j, and stocks: K_j, R_j, W_j. Only one set of quantities, namely, fluxes can be estimated directly. The other quantities: stocks ought to be calculated. But it does not mean that stocks are theoretical constructions: they are realities which can be measured by natural units of products. Formulae 2.10 – 2.12 allow us to estimate amounts of stocks in value units.

Formulae 2.13 – 2.15 give the basis for approximate formulae, according to which separate parts of the national wealth can be estimated. For the simple case of four-sector system, one have equations for three components of national wealth: stock of basic production equipment K; residential wealth W; and stock of knowledge and projects R

$$K(t) \ = \ \int_0^\infty e^{-\mu x} I(t - x)\, dx, \tag{2.17}$$

$$R(t) \ = \ \int_0^\infty e^{-\mu x} H(t - x)\, dx, \tag{2.18}$$

$$W(t) \ = \ \int_0^\infty e^{-\mu x} J(t - x)\, dx. \tag{2.19}$$

Material and non-material parts of the wealth of the US at $\mu = 0$ (gross capital) and at $\mu \neq 0$ (pure capital) were estimated by Kendrick (1976). For illustration, the parts of national wealth of the US are shown in Fig. 7. The time dependence of basic production capital can be approximated by exponential function

$$K = 2.42 \times 10^{12} \cdot e^{0.0427\, t} \ \ dollar(1990), \tag{2.20}$$

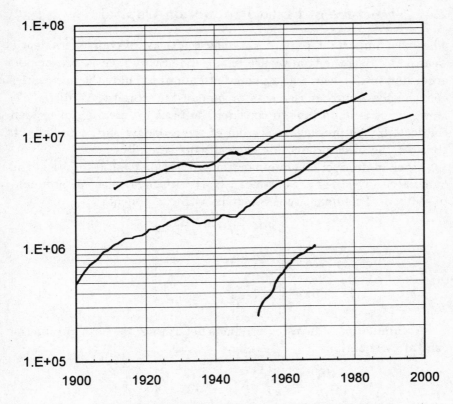

Figure 7 Constituents of the US national wealth

Estimates of value of material national wealth $K+W$ (upper curve) and value of basic production (non-residential) capital K (middle curve) are given according to Survey of Current Business 1990, vol. 70, No 10, p. 32. Estimates of value of developed principles of organisation R (lower curve) are due to Kendrick (1976, Table B-23). All quantities in dollars of year 1990.

where time t is measured in years, whereas $t = 0$ corresponds to year 1950.

We can see that value of non-material wealth, including the value of science, research and projects, is essential and cannot be ignored. Note, that we do not include material belongings of humans into R. It ought to be included in W.

2.4   Structure of Fixed Production Capital

The most important part of national wealth is, of course, residential wealth W. It is the true wealth of society. 'Every man is rich or poor according to the degree in which he can afford to enjoy the necessaries, conveniences, and amusements of human life' (Smith, 1776, p. 47). However, it is important to consider the basis for creating of residential wealth, the production system of the economy and, especially, to consider the basic production capital more carefully.

Stock of production equipment or production capital represents accumulated investment. So, we can start with investment of product j in sector i. This quantity is a matrix with components I_j^i

$$
\mathsf{I} = \left\|
\begin{array}{cccc}
I_1^1 & I_1^2 & \dots & I_1^n \\
I_2^1 & I_2^2 & \dots & I_2^n \\
\dots & \dots & \dots & \dots \\
I_n^1 & I_n^2 & \dots & I_n^n
\end{array}
\right\|.
$$

Accumulation of invested products determines the basic production capital by equations

$$
\frac{dK_j^i}{dt} = I_j^i - \mu K_j^i, \quad i,j = 1,2,...,n, \tag{2.21}
$$

where K_j^i stands for value of basic production equipment of the sort j in the sector i. One can see that the basic production equipment can be considered to be a matrix with components K_j^i

$$
\mathsf{K} = \left\|
\begin{array}{cccc}
K_1^1 & K_1^2 & \dots & K_1^n \\
K_2^1 & K_2^2 & \dots & K_2^n \\
\dots & \dots & \dots & \dots \\
K_n^1 & K_n^2 & \dots & K_n^n
\end{array}
\right\|.
$$

We can define investment and total amount of product of the sort j in all sectors as

$$
I_j = \sum_{i=1}^{n} I_j^i, \quad K_j = \sum_{i=1}^{n} K_j^i, \quad j = 1,2,...,n. \tag{2.22}
$$

Quite analogically, we can define gross investment of all products in sector i and total amount of the basic production capital in this sector

$$I^i = \sum_{j=1}^{n} I_j^i, \quad K^i = \sum_{j=1}^{n} K_j^i, \quad i = 1, 2, ..., n. \qquad (2.23)$$

One can sum equation 2.21 over suffixes i or j to obtain equations for dynamics of the total amount of equipment labelled j and for dynamics of fixed sectoral capital, correspondingly

$$\frac{dK_j}{dt} = I_j - \mu K_j, \quad j = 1, 2, ..., n, \qquad (2.24)$$

$$\frac{dK^i}{dt} = I^i - \mu K^i, \quad i = 1, 2, ..., n.$$

The gross investment into the whole production system and basic production capital of the whole economy are now defined as

$$I = \sum_{i=1}^{n} I^i = \sum_{j=1}^{n} I_j = \sum_{i,j=1}^{n} I_j^i,$$

$$K = \sum_{i=1}^{n} K^i = \sum_{j=1}^{n} K_j = \sum_{i,j=1}^{n} K_j^i. \qquad (2.25)$$

Equation 2.21 determines a time structure of production capital

$$K_j^i(t) = \int_0^\infty e^{-\mu x} I_j^i(t - x) \, dx. \qquad (2.26)$$

One can see that the quantity

$$k_j^i(t, t - x) = e^{-\mu x} I_j^i(t - x) \qquad (2.27)$$

is a part of the existing fixed production capital which was introduced during a unit of time at the moment of time $t - x$. The quantity 2.27 is the smallest part of capital which can be considered in macroeconomic theory.

2.5   Mechanism of Exchange and Scale of Value

The input-output model of the production system of economy assumes that the specific motion takes place: natural substances transform into finished and semi-finished things, the latter transform into other things and so on, until all this is consumed finally, and substances return into the environment as waste. From the other side, the transformations of products in an economy can be described as fluxes of value which appears at the first touching the substance with the hand of human being, moves together with material substance of a product, leaving its material form, transfers into other substances, and disappears at final consumption. However, to discuss a mechanism of movement of products, we need to consider human beings, their desire to consume and, consequently, to produce. In developed societies, man consumes not only those products which he produces. So, exchange of products which, in fact, is the exchange of efforts, is a general phenomenon in modern societies.

One can rarely find barter exchange in the modern societies. Man exchanges his services for *money*, and, then, can exchange the money for products he wants. As a medium of exchange, money must be held between exchangers and thus exists as a separate product. Early moneys took the form of different commodities, such as animals, furs, silver, gold, and so on. The modern money is paper money and considered as separate product. This product is circulating in the economy, providing exchange of products. The modern money is inherently useless. The value of modern money derives only from the fact that it can be exchanged for the product. Money is a certificate that its owner has a right to get a certain set of products.

Money exists as far as there is a demand for money. Any arbitrary amount (in money units) of the circulating money M in coins, bank notes and cashing deposits can be introduced in the system. A money scale of value, that is, money expression of unit of value depends on the value to be represented by this amount of money, say, on value of the final output Y or part of it. Money gives an estimation of value. As a scale of value, price index ρ is usually used. The price index is not a constant but apparently depends on the amount of the circulating money M (in money units) which set against a set of products with value Y. So, three quantities: M, ρ and Y are connected with each other and the amount of money can be written as increasing function of ρ and Y

$$M = M(\rho, Y) \tag{2.28}$$

or, taking dimension of the quantities into account,

$$M = \theta\rho Y, \tag{2.29}$$

where coefficient θ has a sense of a mean time from production to consumption of final product. This quantity is a characteristic of the system and does not depend on the amount of the circulating money M (at large M). The quantity reverse to θ is a velocity of circulation of money. Relation 2.29 is an expression of so-called *quantity theory of money* which, according to Harrod (1969, p. 26) was classically exposed in the report of the British Bullion Committee (1810).[2]

Equation 2.29 is valid for steady-state or *equilibrium* situations.[3] In non-equilibrium situations, every variable lives on its own. The system can generate its own money or hide it, so that the total amount of money, as well as the price index, remains an uncertain quantity. However, the approach to equilibrium point can be described by the simple equations

$$\frac{dM}{dt} = -a\left(M - \theta\,\rho Y\right), \quad \frac{d\rho}{dt} = -b\left(\rho - \frac{M}{\theta Y}\right). \tag{2.30}$$

Coefficients a and b determine mode and velocity of movement of the system at equilibrium point. One can guess that these quantities are connected with customers' and governmental reaction. For the

---

[2]Further on, Harrod writes: 'Of course, the Bullion Committee did not invent the quantity theory. Traces of it may be found in writers dating back for centuries before that.'

[3]Economic equilibrium assumes that all macroeconomic variables which define economic system are constant, to say nothing of fluctuations. It reminds the definition of equilibrium in thermodynamics: all thermodynamic variables are constant on average, though there is movement of constituent particles of the thermodynamic system. Similarly, material constituent of economic system at equilibrium is not in thermodynamic equilibrium: there are processes of production and consumption of products. Economic equilibrium is an idealisation of reality which was stressed many times (Kornai, 1975), nevertheless it is a very useful idealisation, as well as thermodynamic equilibrium in physics.

equilibrium point to be stable, it is necessary to assume that a and b are positive. However, phenomenon of hyperinflation shows us that one of the coefficients or both of them could be non-positive. Money is usually supplied by a government central bank (Harrod, 1969). The amount of supplied money is usually controlled by a government which might have its own reasons to print money. Nevertheless, the government's task is to keep stability, so it has to react inversely to change of the price index ρ. One can see that stability of equilibrium depends on the mode of government reaction to change of situation.

So, money and price index have to be variables of the theory of economic development. However, we shall simplify the problem, assuming in the following Chapters that value of products is measured by constant money scale.

3 Linear Model of Production System

From material point of view, the process of production is process of transformation of raw materials into finished and semi-finished goods, semi-finished goods into other semi-finished and finished goods and so on, until the finished commodities can be used by human beings. We can observe how clay transforms into pots, how clay, sand, and stone transform into buildings, how ores and raw materials transform into a car.

A method of producing is *technology* which determines, first of all, what one needs to produce this or that thing, determines the material side of process of production. One knows (Leontief, 1936, 1941, 1988), that production system of economy can be divided into many sectors. There are product transfers from sectors to sectors which can be described and material balance ought be observed. This is a material constituent of technology which is reflected in balance equations 2.3 and 2.4 for the variables: gross and final sector outputs: X_j and Y_j and intermediate production consumption X_j^i. One can reduce the number of variables, by introducing quantities which are characteristics of technology of production system, namely, fundamental technological matrices (see equations 3.1 – 3.4). They do not depend on output and are material parameters of production system.

The dynamic equations for input-output model, written in this Chapter, are based on the balance equations and contain investments as a moving force. In this Chapter, investments are determined for the case, when internal restrictions for development are only taken into account. In this case *potential investments* can be defined. The restrictions imposed by labour and energy will be introduced in the subsequent Chapters and we return to multi-sector dynamic equations in Chapter 8.

3.1 Fundamental Technological Matrices

The balance relation, namely, equation 2.3 and 2.4 which were written in the previous Chapter do not allow us to determine the output of the production system of economy without extra suggestion. It is necessary to discuss some further assumptions to connect the intermediate production consumption X_j^i and fixed production capital K_j^i with gross sector output X_j. Further on, we consider the simplest case of linear approximation which was proposed and investigated by Leontief (1936, 1941). This approximation is valid for the essentially aggregated description.

Two technological matrices can be introduced by the relations

$$\frac{dX_j^i}{dt} = a_j^i \frac{dX_i}{dt},$$
(3.1)

$$\frac{dK_j^i}{dt} = b_j^i \frac{dX_i}{dt}.$$
(3.2)

The first relation defines matrix of intermediate consumption coefficients (input-output matrix), and the second one defines matrix of fixed capital coefficients (capital-output matrix), correspondingly,

$$A = \begin{Vmatrix} a_1^1 & a_1^2 & \cdots & a_1^n \\ a_2^1 & a_2^2 & \cdots & a_2^n \\ \cdots & \cdots & \cdots & \cdots \\ a_n^1 & a_n^2 & \cdots & a_n^n \end{Vmatrix}, \quad B = \begin{Vmatrix} b_1^1 & b_1^2 & \cdots & b_1^n \\ b_2^1 & b_2^2 & \cdots & b_2^n \\ \cdots & \cdots & \cdots & \cdots \\ b_n^1 & b_n^2 & \cdots & b_n^n \end{Vmatrix}.$$

Of course, in the case when components of matrices do not depend on time, relations 3.1 and 3.2 reduce to the following ones

$$X_j^i = a_j^i X_i,$$
(3.3)

$$K_j^i = b_j^i X_i.$$
(3.4)

By equations 3.1 and 3.2, the of components of technological matrices A and B are characteristics of technology which is introduced at given moment of time, whereas the components, determined by equations 3.3 and 3.4 represent a mixture of all technologies, old and new. It is preferable to use the definition 3.1 and 3.2, though the difference can be negligible if technology changes slowly. It is naturally to suppose that all components of matrices A and B are non-negative. It follows also from productivity condition (see the next Section) that components of matrix A are less than unity.

Matrices A and B are characteristic of technology introduced into production system. To estimate of components of the matrices, one ought to apply to empirical data and to use statistical methods of evaluation. As an example, the result of an estimation of matrices for the production system, consisting of four sectors, which were described in Sector 2.1, are demonstrated further on

$$
A \;=\; \left\| \begin{array}{cccc}
0.187 & 0.172 & 0.103 & 0.0356 \\
0.071 & 0.092 & 0.053 & 0.0178 \\
0.0201 & 0.0102 & 0.0451 & 0.0134 \\
0 & 0 & 0 & 0
\end{array} \right\| , \tag{3.5}
$$

$$
B \;=\; \left\| \begin{array}{cccc}
0 & 0 & 0 & 0 \\
0.83 & 0.45 & 2.34 & 2.18 \\
0.01 & 0.097 & 0.90 & 0.214 \\
0 & 0 & 0 & 0
\end{array} \right\| \quad year. \tag{3.6}
$$

To approach reality, the data for Soviet Union economy in year 1987 were used (Narodnoje Khozjaistvo, 1988). Nevertheless, the estimates is quite uncertain, so this example can be used as an illustrative example only.

Note that matrices A and B, as it is seen from example 3.5 and 3.6 are degenerate. This is not the exception but the rule.

3.2 Dynamic Relations in Linear Approximation

Now , we return to the balance relations 2.3 and 2.4. We use formulae 3.1 and 3.2 to rewrite the balance relations in the form

$$
\frac{dX_j}{dt} \;=\; \sum_{i=1}^{n} a_j^i \frac{dX_i}{dt} + \frac{dY_j}{dt}, \tag{3.7}
$$

$$
\frac{dX_i}{dt} \;=\; a^i \frac{dX_i}{dt} + \frac{dZ^i}{dt}, \tag{3.8}
$$

$$
a^i \;=\; \sum_{l=1}^{n} a_l^i. \tag{3.9}
$$

One can consider requirement of productivity in the form that rate of sector production of value has to be non-negative, that is,

$$\frac{dZ^i}{dt} \geq 0$$

which, with help of equation 3.8, determines

$$\sum_{l=1}^{n} a_l^i < 1, \quad i = 1, 2, ..., n.$$

So as each component of matrix A is non-negative, one has

$$a_j^i < 1, \quad i, j = 1, 2, ..., n. \tag{3.10}$$

To obtain a new form of dynamic equation for output, we start with equation 2.21 and, using definition 3.2, have

$$b_j^i \frac{dX_i}{dt} = I_j^i - \mu K_j^i, \quad i, j = 1, 2, ..., n. \tag{3.11}$$

One can see that value of the stock of production equipment or capital K_j^i cannot be expressed through gross output X_i in a simple way, so that we ought to keep equation 2.21 in line with equation 3.11. These equations together determine gross output X_i, if we consider investment I_j^i to be given as function of time.

The other two quantities K^i and K_j, defined by relations 2.24 are of interest here. We shall demonstrate that they will appear to be connected with each other by means of components of matrix B.

We can sum equation 3.11 over suffix j and, in accordance with definitions 2.23, obtain

$$b^i \frac{dX_i}{dt} = I^i - \mu K^i, \quad b^i = \sum_{l=1}^{n} b_l^i, \quad i = 1, 2, ..., n. \tag{3.12}$$

On the other hand, summing equation 3.11 over suffix i, we obtain another set of equations

$$\sum_{i=1}^{n} b_j^i \frac{dX_i}{dt} = I_j - \mu K_j, \quad j = 1, 2, ..., n. \tag{3.13}$$

Then, we can exclude the derivatives from relations 3.12 and 3.13 to obtain

$$\sum_{i=1}^{n} \bar{b}_j^i (I^i - \mu K^i) = I_j - \mu K_j,$$

where a dimensionless matrix of capital coefficients is introduced

$$\bar{b}_j^i = (b^i)^{-1} b_j^i. \tag{3.14}$$

In virtue of the arbitrary value of μ, one can obtain the following relations

$$I_j = \sum_{i=1}^{n} \bar{b}_j^i I^i, \quad K_j = \sum_{i=1}^{n} \bar{b}_j^i K^i. \tag{3.15}$$

The approximations made when one obtains these relations are connected with representations of depreciated capital, so we ought to consider relations 3.15 to be valid with only the first terms related with respect to rate of growth.

Note, that components of dimensionless matrix of capital coefficients cannot be arbitrary. First of all, by virtue of definition, components of dimentionless stock matrix 3.14 are connected by relations

$$\sum_{j=1}^{n} \bar{b}_j^i = 1, \quad i = 1, 2, ..., n. \tag{3.16}$$

Apart from this, one can find one more relation between components. This is originated from the obvious relation

$$\sum_{j=1}^{n} I_j = \sum_{i=1}^{n} I^i$$

which, making use of formula 3.15, can be rewritten as

$$\sum_{i,j=1}^{n} (\bar{b}_j^i - \delta_j^i) I^i = 0.$$

One can see that a non-zero vector of investment I^i exists, if the following sufficient condition is valid

$$|\bar{b}_j^i - \delta_j^i| = 0. \tag{3.17}$$

As an example, we write down a matrix of capital coefficients for four-sector model

$$
\bar{b}_j^i = \left\|
\begin{array}{cccc}
0 & 0 & 0 & 0 \\
0.99 & 0.930 & 0.722 & 0.911 \\
0.01 & 0.070 & 0.278 & 0.089 \\
0 & 0 & 0 & 0
\end{array}
\right\| .
$$

3.3 Effects of Prices

Though the prices are not shown explicitly in relations 3.7 and 3.8, they are written at implicit assumption that price of each product is given and unchanged. However, in no case, the prices are fixed: the prices can change, and, so, we ought to investigate the effect of price changes on the written relations.

We assume that there is a reference state with set of the prices, which are considered to be all equal to unity, and an arbitrary state with a given set of prices, so that components of output in the reference (with sign ˆ) and the arbitrary state are connected by relations

$$
X_i = p_i \hat{X}_i, \quad Y_i = p_i \hat{Y}_i, \quad i = 1, 2, ..., n, \tag{3.18}
$$

where p_i is the price index in arbitrary state.

Then, equation 3.7 can be rewritten in the form

$$
p_j \frac{d\hat{X}_j}{dt} + \hat{X}_j \frac{dp_j}{dt} = \sum_{i=1}^{n} a_j^i \left(p_i \frac{d\hat{X}_i}{dt} + \hat{X}_i \frac{dp_i}{dt} \right) + p_j \frac{dY_j}{dt} + \hat{Y}_j \frac{dp_j}{dt}.
$$

One ought to accept that balance equation has the same form for any system of prices. So, one ought to write down two separate relations: balance equation, which has the form of equation 3.7, and an equation for prices

$$
\frac{d\hat{X}_j}{dt} = \sum_{i=1}^{n} \hat{a}_j^i \frac{d\hat{X}_i}{dt} + \frac{d\hat{Y}_j}{dt}, \tag{3.19}
$$

$$
\hat{X}_j \frac{d\ln p_j}{dt} = \sum_{i=1}^{n} \hat{a}_j^i \hat{X}_i \frac{d\ln p_i}{dt} + \hat{Y}_j \frac{d\ln p_j}{dt}, \tag{3.20}
$$

where

$$\hat{a}_j^i = a_j^i \frac{p_i}{p_j}, \quad a_j^i = \hat{a}_j^i \frac{p_j}{p_i}. \tag{3.21}$$

Relation 3.20 can be considered, as a set of equations for quantities

$$\frac{d \ln p_i}{dt}, \quad i = 1, 2, ..., n$$

which can have a non-trivial solution, if the following condition is fulfilled

$$\left| (\delta_j^i - a_j^i) X_i - Y_j \delta_j^i \right| = 0. \tag{3.22}$$

If a_j^i does not depend on time, condition 3.22 is always valid, otherwise, condition 3.22 is a condition for the rates of growth of components a_j^i.

So, one can see that the prices of products cannot be quite arbitrary quantities. A non-trivial solution of set 3.20 determines a relation between prices of different products.

Now, taking the previous formulae into account, relation 3.8 can be written in the form

$$\frac{dZ^i}{dt} = (1 - a^i) \left(p_i \frac{d\hat{X}_i}{dt} + \hat{X}_i \frac{dp_i}{dt} \right). \tag{3.23}$$

The rate of sector production of value is divided into two parts: the rate connected with a change of gross output in 'natural' units and the rate connected with a change of the price.

We consider a sector as an economic subject who plans its activity and can take decision about amount of gross output. The aim of the sector is to obtain a bigger amount of production of value Z^j. We can believe that increase of output is stimulated by increase of production of value in sector. In the simplest case

$$\frac{d\hat{X}_i}{dt} = k_i \frac{dZ^i}{dt}, \tag{3.24}$$

where k_i $(i = 1, 2, ..., n)$ are the sensibility coefficients. The coefficient k_i shows how sector i reacts on the increase of production of value. We consider k_i to be non-negative and limited due to the possibilities of production

$$k_i < \frac{1}{(1 - a^i)p_i}. \tag{3.25}$$

Relations 3.23 and 3.24 determine rate of sector production of value

$$\frac{dZ^i}{dt} = \frac{(1-a^i)X_i}{[1-k_i(1-a^i)p_i]p_i}\frac{dp_i}{dt}. \tag{3.26}$$

From this relation using relations 3.7 and 3.8, one can obtain formulae for rate of gross and final products of the sector

$$\frac{dX_i}{dt} = \frac{X_i}{[1-k_i(1-a^i)p_i]p_i}\frac{dp_i}{dt}, \quad i=1,2,...,n, \tag{3.27}$$

$$\frac{dY_j}{dt} = \sum_{i=1}^{n}\frac{(\delta_j^i - a_j^i)X_i}{[1-k_i(1-a^i)p_i]p_i}\frac{dp_i}{dt}, \quad j=1,2,...,n. \tag{3.28}$$

The last expression defines the partial derivatives of the function $Y_j = Y_j(p_1, p_2, ..., p_n)$ which is called the supply function as

$$\frac{\partial Y_j}{\partial p_i} = \frac{(\delta_j^i - a_j^i)X_i}{[1-k_i(1-a^i)p_i]p_i}. \tag{3.29}$$

One can see that final output of a sector is an increasing function of the price of its own product, and a decreasing function of prices of all other products.

Note, that it is convenient to rewrite relation 3.18 in the vector form

$$\mathsf{X} = \mathsf{P}\hat{\mathsf{X}}, \quad \hat{\mathsf{X}} = \mathsf{P}^{-1}\mathsf{X}, \qquad \mathsf{Y} = \mathsf{P}\hat{\mathsf{Y}}, \quad \hat{\mathsf{Y}} = \mathsf{P}^{-1}\mathsf{Y}, \tag{3.30}$$

where the transformation matrixes are introduced

$$\mathsf{P} = \left\| \begin{matrix} p_1 & 0 & \cdots & 0 \\ 0 & p_2 & \cdots & 0 \\ \cdots & \cdots & \cdots & \cdots \\ 0 & 0 & \cdots & p_n \end{matrix} \right\|, \quad \mathsf{P}^{-1} = \left\| \begin{matrix} p_1^{-1} & 0 & \cdots & 0 \\ 0 & p_2^{-1} & \cdots & 0 \\ \cdots & \cdots & \cdots & \cdots \\ 0 & 0 & \cdots & p_n^{-1} \end{matrix} \right\|. \tag{3.31}$$

Then, relations 3.21 for transformation of the technological matrix can be written as

$$\mathsf{A} = \mathsf{P}\hat{\mathsf{A}}\mathsf{P}^{-1}, \quad \hat{\mathsf{A}} = \mathsf{P}^{-1}\mathsf{A}\mathsf{P}. \tag{3.32}$$

It is easy to see that analogous relations are valid for matrix of capital coefficients

$$B = P\hat{B}P^{-1}, \quad \hat{B} = P^{-1}BP. \tag{3.33}$$

One calls matrices $\hat{A}$ and A, also as matrices $\hat{B}$ and B similar matrices (Korn and Korn, 1968). To separate changes of matrices which are connected with technology changes from changes influenced by price changes, one has to consider some invariant combinations of components of the matrices. It is known that similar matrices have the same eigenvalues which thus, do not depend on the prices.

3.4 Leontief Equations

The relations given in the previous Sections allow one to write down the equations for gross and final outputs at given matrixes A and B as functions of time. The situation becomes much simpler, if one assumes that time dependence of matrices can be neglected. In this case one can rewrite equation 3.7 to obtain the Leontief static equation

$$X_j = \sum_{i=1}^{n} a_j^i X_i + Y_j, \quad j = 1, 2, ..., n. \tag{3.34}$$

A solution of this equation allows one to plan the gross output X_j which is needed to get the final output Y_j at a given technology. Both X_j and Y_j in equation 3.34 are referred to the same moment of time.

To obtain an equation for gross output as a function of time, we refer to equation 3.13 which, with help of equation 3.4, can be written in the form

$$\sum_{i=1}^{n} b_j^i \frac{dX_i}{dt} = I_j - \mu \sum_{i=1}^{n} b_j^i X_i, \quad j = 1, 2, ..., n. \tag{3.35}$$

Gross investment of product j in all sectors I_j are determined by relation 2.8 as

$$I_j = Y_j - C_j - H_j, \quad j = 1, 2, ..., n, \tag{3.36}$$

where $C_j = J_j + \Pi_j$ is the total personal consumption of product j.

The last relation allows us to rewrite equation 3.35 in the following form

$$\sum_{i=1}^{n} b_j^i \frac{dX_i}{dt} = Y_j - C_j - H_j - \mu \sum_{i=1}^{n} b_j^i X_i, \quad j = 1, 2, ..., n. \quad (3.37)$$

Now we can introduce new characteristics of the system, to define unknown quantities through gross output

$$C_j + H_j = \sum_{i=1}^{n} c_j^i X_i, \quad j = 1, 2, ..., n. \quad (3.38)$$

Components of consumption matrix c_j^i are considered to be non-negative and constant. Besides, one can easily see that following relation is valid

$$\sum_{i=1}^{n} c_j^i \leq 1, \quad j = 1, 2, ..., n.$$

One can use equation 3.34, to determine the final output Y_j and to obtain

$$X_j = \sum_{i=1}^{n} \left(a_j^i X_i + c_j^i X_i + b_j^i \frac{dX_i}{dt} + \mu b_j^i X_i \right), \quad j = 1, 2, ..., n. \quad (3.39)$$

This is the dynamical equation for gross sectoral output which was derived by Leontief (1941). One believes that equation 3.39 is applicable to the real system, if changes of matrices A and B due to the technological changes can be neglected. Further on in this section it is convenient to use a vector form of the equation 3.39

$$B \frac{dX}{dt} = (E - A - \mu B - C)X. \quad (3.40)$$

In the considered case, when all parameters in equations 3.39 and 3.40 are constant, gross output can be found in the form

$$X_j(t) = X_j(0)e^{\sigma t}, \quad (3.41)$$

where $X_j(0)$ satisfy the set of algebraic equations

$$[E - A - (\mu + \sigma)B - C]X(0) = 0. \quad (3.42)$$

This is a trajectory of balanced growth, when rates of growth of gross output in all sectors are the same.

There are not-trivial solutions of equations 3.42, if the determinator of the system is equal to zero, that is,

$$|E - A - (\mu + \sigma)B - C| = 0. \tag{3.43}$$

This condition determines the rate of gross output σ as function of components of matrices A, B, and C. As far as matrix B is degenerate, the number of values of σ is less than the number of variables n. So, for example, for the above described four sector model, for which matrices A and B are given by 3.5 and 3.6, equation 3.43 determines two values of σ, whereas the biggest one corresponds to negative initial values of some variables, so that the only one ought to be considered. The rate of growth depends on the components of matrices A, B and C and has the biggest value about 0.2 when components of consumption matrix and coefficients of storage of intermediate products are equal to zero. Of course, this potential value exceeds the real rates of growth.

Note that some technical difficulties can appear when one tries to calculate the rates of growth from equation 3.43 at big values of n. So, specially developed methods (von Neumann, 1937) are used for this aim (Cheremnykh, 1982).

To apply these methods to equations 3.39, one can consider them in moments of time $t = 0, 1, 2, \ldots$ and assume

$$X_i = X_i(t), \qquad \frac{dX_i}{dt} = X_i(t+1) - X_i(t)$$

which implies

$$\sum_{i=1}^{n} b_j^i X_i(t+1) = \sum_{i=1}^{n} \left(\delta_j^i - a_j^i + (1 - \mu)b_j^i - c_j^i \right) X_i, \quad j = 1, 2, \ldots, n.$$

This equations can be rewritten in the form of inequality

$$\alpha B X \leq (E - A - (\mu + \sigma)B - C)X, \tag{3.44}$$

if one can introduce the ratio of growth

$$\alpha = \min_{i=1 \div n} \frac{X_i(t+1)}{X_i(t)}.$$

This quantity depends on the vector X which can be chosen in such a way that α would take the greatest value

$$\hat{\alpha} = \max_{\mathsf{X}} \alpha(\mathsf{X}).$$

This ratio determines the optional balance trajectory of the quickest growth

$$X_i(t) = X_i(0)\hat{\alpha}^t = X_i(0)e^{\sigma t}. \tag{3.45}$$

3.5   General Dynamics and Potential Investment

Now, in contrast to the previous Section, we shall apply the theory to a general case when components of technological matrices A and B are assumed to be functions of time. From combination of formulae 3.2 and 3.7, one can see that final output can be written as

$$\frac{dY_j}{dt} = \sum_{i=1}^{n} \xi_j^i \frac{dK^i}{dt}, \quad \xi_j^i = \frac{\delta_j^i - a_j^i}{b^i}, \tag{3.46}$$

where a matrix of marginal productivities of sectoral capital with components ξ_j^i is introduced. For simple four-sector model of the production system, components of the matrix of capital marginal productivities can be found from values 3.5 and 3.6 as

$$\Xi = \left\|\begin{array}{cccc} 0.968 & -0.313 & -0.0318 & -0.0149 \\ -0.0845 & 1.65 & -0.0164 & -0.0745 \\ -0.0239 & -0.0185 & 0.295 & -0.00561 \\ 0 & 0 & 0 & 0.418 \end{array}\right\| \; year^{-1}. \tag{3.47}$$

One adds one of relations 2.24 to 3.46 to obtain a set of equations

$$\frac{dY_j}{dt} = \sum_{i=1}^{n} \xi_j^i (I^i - \mu K^i), \tag{3.48}$$

$$\frac{dK^i}{dt} = I^i - \mu K^i,$$

where sectoral investments I^i are calculated according to formulae 3.15 and 3.36 from a system of algebraic equations

$$\sum_{i=1}^{n} \bar{b}_j^i I^i = Y_j - C_j - H_j. \qquad (3.49)$$

We can assume that storage H_j and consumption C_j have to be non-negative and to have reasonable values, while they are under control of society and are given as function of time. Besides, some of the components C_j are identically equal to zero. We omit the storage of all products, apart from the principles of organisation, and take into account the degeneracy of matrix B to rewrite relations 3.49 in the form

$$Y_j \geq 0 \qquad for \quad resource \quad products, \qquad (3.50)$$

$$Y_j \geq \sum_{i=1}^{n} \bar{b}_j^i I^i \qquad for \quad investment \quad products, \qquad (3.51)$$

$$Y_j \geq H_j \qquad for \quad principles \quad of \quad organisation, \qquad (3.52)$$

$$Y_j \geq C_j \qquad for \quad final \quad products. \qquad (3.53)$$

We assume here that there is no restriction due to material resources and no other restrictions.

Potential investments $\tilde{I}^i$ ought to be found as the values from a solutions of equations 3.50 – 3.53, that is,

$$Y_j = 0 \qquad for \quad resource \quad products, \qquad (3.54)$$

$$Y_j = \sum_{i=1}^{n} \bar{b}_j^i I^i \qquad for \quad investment \quad products, \qquad (3.55)$$

$$Y_j = H_j \qquad for \quad principles \quad of \quad organisation, \qquad (3.56)$$

$$Y_j = C_j \qquad for \quad final \quad products. \qquad (3.57)$$

Equation 3.55 does not determine sectoral investment in a unique way: the number of equations is less than the number of variables. As for equations 3.54 and 3.56 – 3.57, they do not contain investments.[1]

We have to complete system 3.55 or to use an extra condition to determine the sectoral investments. For example, we can require that the rate of final product ought to be a maximum, that is,

$$\max \sum_{i=1}^{n} \xi^i \left(I^i - \mu K^i \right), \quad \xi^i = \sum_{j=1}^{n} \xi_j^i, \tag{3.58}$$

while relations 3.51 ought to be considered as restrictions. Instead of 3.51, one can use the restriction which follows equation 3.49

$$\sum_{i=1}^{n} I^i \leq Y - C, \quad Y - C = \sum_{j=1}^{n} (Y_j - C_j). \tag{3.59}$$

In this way, the final product and final consumption determine the potential investments

$$\tilde{I}^i = \tilde{I}^i(\xi^i, Y - C). \tag{3.60}$$

Together with equations 3.48, potential investments determine a trajectory of the largest potential growth. The problem can be solved by numerical methods, while the maximisation problem 3.58 – 3.59 has to be solved by standard methods of linear programming on every step of solution of the Cauchy problem.

However, instead of described procedure of calculation of potential investment, some other procedures can be invented to determine unambiguously the trajectory of evolution from the written equations. We ought to know, for example, a form of trajectory of evolution. We

---

[1]One can increase the number of equations, if one uses equation 3.57 in the form

$$Y_j = c_j \sum_{i=1}^{n} L^j.$$

This relationship has to be differentiated, to obtain

$$\frac{dY_j}{dt} = \dot{c}_j \sum_{i=1}^{n} L^i + c_j \sum_{i=1}^{n} \frac{dL^i}{dt}.$$

Now we can use definition of derivative of final output and labour from equations 8.1 and 8.4 and obtain a few equations for sectoral investment.

can say about any extra condition which one needs to determine a trajectory of evolution as about principle of development. In the considered case, the principle of development is that the society manages its resources in the best way.

In this Section we assumed that the final consumption and the storage of intermediate products are given; in this case the potential investment $\tilde{I}^i$ can be determined. In more general case, availability of labour and energy impose some strong restrictions on the development of the production system and ought to be included into the theory. Real investments appears to be no more than potential investments $\tilde{I}^i$ determined from the above equations. The final consumption and the storage of intermediate products appear to be consequence of evolution of the system. We shall discuss the question in the subsequent Chapters and return to the multi-sector equations in Chapter 8.

3.6   Enterprise and Basic Technological Processes

From a microeconomic point of view, production system consists of numerous enterprises, each of them including one or more *basic technological processes*. Exactly, the latter can be considered as *atoms* of production system. Methods to describe the resources of an enterprise consisting of a finite or an infinite set of basic technological processes were proposed by von Neumann (1937) and Gale (1960), respectfully. We shall consider a finite set of basic technological processes, namely, the von Neumann model of enterprise.

Every enterprise produces one or several products , whereas it consumes some products. In other words, the enterprise transforms the input set of products $x_j, x_i, \ldots$, where labels of products $j, i, \ldots$ are fixed, in an output set: $x_l, x_m, \ldots$, where labels of products $l, m, \ldots$ are also fixed. It is convenient to introduce the input and output vectors u and v with non-negative components u_k and v_k, $k = 1, 2, \ldots, n$. Some of components are equal to zero.

We assume that components of vectors are measured in units of value, so the final output of the enterprise is

$$y = \sum_{j=1}^{n} (v_j - u_j). \tag{3.61}$$

This is a contribution of the enterprise in the gross national product.

A couple of vectors (u,v) characterise the technology used in production or, to put it differently, technological process is given as a couple of vectors (u,v). Technological process can be depicted as a point in Euclidean space of dimension $2n$ (Fig. 8).

One can assume that there are basic technological processes, each of which cannot be divided and changed as, for example, a car assembly line. Its characteristic are constant. The only action the manager can do is to switch the line on and off. One can assume that the enterprise consists of a set of the basic technological processes which can be used in different combinations, so that technological process of the enterprise can be represented as an expansion over the basic technological processes

$$(\mathsf{u},\mathsf{v}) = \sum_{j=1}^{r} (\mathsf{a}^j, \mathsf{h}^j) z_j, \tag{3.62}$$

where $z_j \geq 0$ is the intensity of the use of the basic technological process labelled j.

At given basic technological processes and arbitrary vector $\mathsf{z} = (z_1, z_2, \ldots, z_r)$, relation 3.62 determines possible technological processes of the enterprise, that is, a technological set which is a specific characteristic of the enterprise.

The task of the enterprise and of an investigator of the enterprise is to find such a value of z that final output 3.61 would have taken the greatest value.

It is convenient to use a representation for the components of the input and output vectors

$$u_i = \sum_{j=1}^{r} a_i^j z_j, \quad v_i = \sum_{j=1}^{r} h_i^j z_j, \tag{3.63}$$

where a_i^j and h_i^j are components of matrices of input and output, A and H, correspondingly. One can say that the Neumann model is given, if matrices A and H are given.

Then, the final output of the enterprise can be written as follows

$$y(\mathsf{z}) = \sum_{i=1}^{n} \sum_{j=1}^{r} (h_i^j - a_i^j) z_j. \tag{3.64}$$

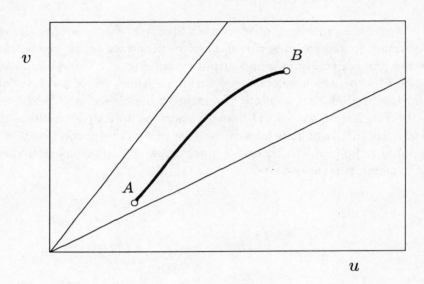

Figure 8 Input-output space

All trajectories are situated (similar to the trajectory AB) inside sector restricted by the straight lines which represent basic technological processes.

One can introduce a potential output-input ratio

$$\alpha(\mathbf{z}) = \min_{j=1,2,\ldots,n;\ v_i \neq 0} \frac{v_i}{u_i} \tag{3.65}$$

which depends on the intensity $\mathbf{z} = (z_1, z_2, \ldots, z_r)$.

So as the final output is non-negative, it follows from relation 3.64

$$\mathbf{Az} \leq \mathbf{Hz}$$

or, using definition 3.65,

$$\alpha\mathbf{Az} \leq \mathbf{Hz}. \tag{3.66}$$

The problem is reduced to finding the greatest rate of growth α. At this condition, the quantity 3.61 would be a maximum as well. The considered problem is mathematically quite similar to the problem discussed in the previous Section (compare equations 3.44 and 3.66).

One can assume that intensity z is a function of time, so that the von Neumann model can describe dynamical processes or, in geometrical terms, the trajectory in input-output space (Fig. 8). If the basic technological processes are unchanged during the time, vector $z = constant$ and the production trajectory is a straight line in technological space – the von Neumann ray. Otherwise, more complicated problems appear. Hundreds of papers were written about the properties of von Neumann-type growth models, golden rules of capital accumulation, turn-pike theorems and so on.

4 Technology and Production Factors

In the previous Chapter, the material side of the production process was described, assuming that a thing can be made from something and there are some tools for making things. In other words, material balance was laid in the basis of description. Now we are going to look at the production process from other point of view. We ought to take into account the energy side of the production process. The role of basic production equipment as a set of sophisticated devices which allow the human being to attract energy from natural sources to the production of commodities is discussed. We use two sets of quantities which, in the macroeconomical approach, reflect the level of technology in the economy: (1) potential rates of growth of production factors $\tilde{\nu}$ and $\tilde{\eta}$ and (2) technological coefficients λ and ε which show how much labour and energy is needed to introduce unit of investment in the production system. The first set of quantities is considered to be exogenous factors in this Chapter, while the second set is connected with internal characteristics of technology. Technological coefficients are very sensitive to technological changes and can be easily estimated on empirical data. As an example, these quantities are estimated for the US economy. Technological coefficients appear to be more appropriate and convenient characteristics of technological changes in economy in comparison with other characteristics.

4.1 Labour and Energy in Production Processes

To produce a good or a service, some work must be done. Modern technologies assume that this work can be done by a human being himself and/or by some external sources, one can say by energy, simultaneously. So, for example, to grind corn into flour a man can use a hand mill, or a water mill, or a wind mill, or a steam mill. The same result can be obtained at different energy consumed and at different labourer's work with which the final result is compared. In the last case a labourer's work is substituted by the work of falling water, or

59

wind, or heat. In these cases, as in many others, production equipment is some means of attracting of external sources (water, wind, coal, oil, et cetera) to the production of things. No matter who or what does the work: the whole work must be done to obtain the final result.[1]

Different mechanisms and appliances are invented to perform the work. Some of these are handled by a man only, some of them allow the man to attract energy from external sources. This is a material realisation of technology, production equipment. Though there are modern descriptions of the role of machinery in production processes (see, for example, a book by Mumford, 1934), we refer to classic description given by Marx (1867, here and later I cite English translation) in chapter XV 'Machinery and Modern Industry' of his famous book:

> On a closer examination of the working machine proper, we find in it, as a general rule, though often, no doubt, under very altered forms, the apparatus and tools used by the handicraftsmen or manufacturing workman: with this difference that instead of being human implements, they are the implements of a mechanism, or mechanical implements (pp. 181-182). The machine proper is therefore a mechanism that, after being set in motion performs with its tools the same operations that were formerly done by the workman with similar tools. Whether the motive power is derived from man or form some other machine, makes no difference in this respect (p. 182). The implements of labour, in the form of machinery, necessitate the substitution of natural forces for human force, and the conscious application of science instead of rule of thumb (p. 188). After making allowance, both in the case of the machine and of the tool, for their average daily cost, that is, for the value they transmit to the product by their average daily wear and tear, and for their consumption of auxiliary substances such as oil, coal and so on, they each do their work gratuitously, just like the forces furnished by nature without the help of man (p. 189).

So, one can see that the main role of the production machine as it is described by Marx (1867), is to attract external sources of energy to production. The substitution of work by external sources for human

---

[1]One can understand work as a process of conversion of energy in technological processes from one form to another, for example, from mechanical into thermic form.

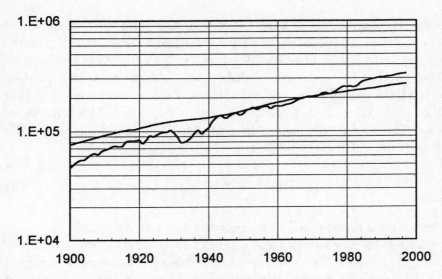

Figure 9 Population and consumption of labour in the US

The smoother curve – population in thousand men. The other curve – consumption of labour in million man-hours per year. The latter dependence can be approximated by exponential function 4.1.

---

work is stressed. The applied technology determines the amount of work of human being L and work of external sources (wind, water, coal,...) E which is necessary for production. Together with production equipment K, these are three main elements which ought to be considered at investigating the production process or technology.

Labour is the most important production factor. Modern technology assumes that man is installed into production process and works inside it. Measure of labour is work (in physical sense, in energy units) done by a labourer. In a sedentary state, the human organism requires about 2500 $kcal/day$ or about 1 $Gcal/year$.[2] Extra activity requires extra supply of energy. Energy needed for working man can be up to two times more than energy needed for a resting man (Rivers and Payne, 1982). So, one can estimate work done by a labourer approximately as 100 $kcal/hour$. Practically, the labour is measured by working time. The most appropriate measure of labour is man-hour, while correc-

---

[2]1 $Gcal = 10^9\ cal.$

tions due to character of labour (heavy or light), intensity of work and other factors are considered to have been taken into account. For the last sentence, I rely on Scott (1989) who in his turn refers to Kendrick (1967) and to Denison with Poullier (1967). As an example, according to the data compiled in Appendix, the amount of man-hours per year (labour) in the economy of the US is shown in Fig. 9 as a function of time. The dependence can be approximated by straight line, especially after year 1950, so for this period

$$L = 1.44 \times 10^{11} \times e^{0.0186\,t} \ man \cdot hour/year, \qquad (4.1)$$

where time t is measured in years, while $t = 0$ at 1950.

Labour can be substituted by energy from external sources in production processes. However, in some technological processes energy is not a substitute. Energy is playing a main role in the production of aluminium, some chemical processes and other. Besides, energy can directly create products (heat, light and so on). Energy is consumed[3] now in great amounts. Consumed energy is useful, as far as it creates products. However, a part of energy appears to be lost for production. One ought to distinguish between primary consumption of energy, that is, consumption of primary sources of energy such as wood, wind, falling water, coal, oil, gas and others, and final production consumption of energy (Paterson, 1996; Nakićenović *et al*, 1996). According to the latter authors, the global average of primary to final efficiency is about 70% in year 1990, while it is higher in developed countries. Data collected by Ayres (1998c, Table 2) demonstrates that efficiency of energy conversion increased during the last centuries. As illustration, Fig. 10 shows the primary – as it is shown in Energy Statistics Books (1993 and other years) – and final calculated consumption of energy in the US economy, while rate of efficiency growth was taken arbitrarily as 1.5%.

---

[3]For the sake of precision the word *consumption* should be replaced by the word *conversion*. Energy cannot be *used up* in production process, it can only be converted into other forms: chemical energy into heat energy, heat energy into mechanical energy, mechanical energy into heat energy and so on. The problems, arising at estimation of amount of energy which is converted (used up) in production processes to do useful work, are discussed by Paterson (1996), Nakićenović *et al* (1996), Zarnikau *et al* (1996) and Ayres (1998a).

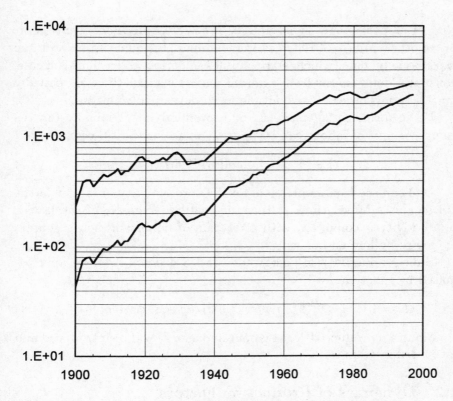

Figure 10 Consumption of energy in the US economy

Primary (upper curve) and final consumption is estimated in million tons of coal equivalent per year. The lower curve can be approximated by exponential function 4.2.

The dependence of final production consumption from year 1950 can be approximated by function

$$E = 413 \times 10^9 \times e^{0.0371\,t} \; kg \; coal \; equivalent/year, \qquad (4.2)$$

where, as in previous examples, time t is measured in years, starting from year 1950.

One can estimate the consumption of energy per labour unit. For the US economy

$$E/L = 2.87 \times e^{0.0185\,t} \; kg \; coal \; equivalent/man \cdot hour.$$

Now (1990) this quantity is 38.6×10^3 *kg coal equivalent/man · year* or, in other units,[4] 30800 *kcal/man · hour*. This quantity exceeds the work done by man, which is about 100 *kcal/man · hour*. This is a rule: consumption of energy from external sources exceeds the work done by man by a few orders of magnitude in all developed countries.

Using formulae 2.7 and 4.1, bulk productivity of labour, that is, value per unit of labour can be approximated for the US economy as

$$Y/L = 11.94 \times e^{0.0122\,t} \; dollar(1990)/man \cdot hour. \qquad (4.3)$$

One can see from expression 4.4 that productivity of labour in the US increases by six times during the century. Increase of the labour productivity is connected with attraction of newer and newer sources of energy by human beings.

Bulk productivity of energy for the US economy can be approximated by function

$$Y/E = 4.16 \times e^{-0.0063\,t} \; dollar(1990)/kg \; coal \; equivalent. \qquad (4.4)$$

Marginal productivities of labour and energy will be introduced and estimated in Chapter 6.

4.2   Dynamics of Production Factors

So, to describe the process of production in a proper way, we ought to take into account fixed production equipment (fixed production capital) and two factors which animate equipment: manpower and external energy. The consumption of labour and energy in the economy can be broken down into amounts of sectoral consumption

$$L = \sum_{i=1}^{n} L^i, \quad E = \sum_{i=1}^{n} E^i. \qquad (4.5)$$

We shall consider a sector, which is characterised by the basic production equipment of the sector K^i and production factors L^i and E^i which are necessary to animate the basic production equipment.

To develop a proper description of a technological process, it is necessary to take into account that different equipment is introduced

---

[4]1 *kg coal equivalent* $= 7000$ *kcal*.

into the production process at different moments in time. So, the age of existing production capital is different and, similar to formula 2.26, we can write down an expression for structure of sector fixed production capital

$$K^i(t) = \int_{-\infty}^{t} k^i(t, s)ds,$$

where $k^i(t, s)$ is the part of fixed capital existing at time t which was introduced at time $t - s$ during unit of time. This quantity is a solution of equation

$$\frac{\partial k^i(t, s)}{\partial t} = -\mu(t, s)k^i(t, s) \tag{4.6}$$

at initial condition

$$k^i(s, s) = I^i(s). \tag{4.7}$$

Then one can integrate expression 4.6 to obtain a law

$$\frac{dK^i}{dt} = I^i - \int_{-\infty}^{t} \mu(t, s)k^i(t, s)ds.$$

From this equation, in the case when coefficient of amortisation μ does not depend on time, one obtains

$$\frac{dK^i}{dt} = I^i - \mu K^i. \tag{4.8}$$

The existing technology determines how many work places and how much energy it is necessary for production mechanism to be in action.

The amount of production factor in sector i can be represented by the formulae

$$L^i(t) = \int_{-\infty}^{t} l^i(t, s)ds, \quad E^i(t) = \int_{-\infty}^{t} e^i(t, s)ds, \tag{4.9}$$

where $l^i(t, s)$ and $e^i(t, s)$ are labour and energy which are necessary for part of fixed capital $k^i(t, s)$ to be in action, so following relations can be written down

$$l^i(t, s) = \lambda^i(s)k^i(t, s), \quad e^i(t, s) = \varepsilon^i(s)k^i(t, s). \tag{4.10}$$

In virtue of relation 4.7

$$l^i(s, s) = \lambda^i(s)\Gamma^i(s), \quad e^i(s, s) = \varepsilon^i(s)\Gamma^i(s), \tag{4.11}$$

where $\Gamma^i(s)$ is gross investment in sector i at time s.

Coefficients $\lambda^i > 0$ and $\varepsilon^i > 0$ determine the required amount of labour and external energy per unit of increase of capital: therefore they can be denominated as labour requirement and energy requirement, correspondingly. The values of these coefficients are determined by applied technology, therefore we shall also call them technological coefficients.

One can see that in virtue of equation 4.6, equations for dynamics of quantities 4.10 can be written as follows:

$$\frac{\partial l^i(t, s)}{\partial t} = -\mu(t, s)l^i(t, s), \quad \frac{\partial e^i(t, s)}{\partial t} = -\mu(t, s)e^i(t, s). \tag{4.12}$$

We can use definitions 4.9 to determine the required amount of the production factors in sector

$$\frac{dL^i}{dt} = \lambda^i\Gamma^i - \int_{-\infty}^t \mu(t, s)l^i(t, s)ds, \quad \frac{dE^i}{dt} = \varepsilon^i\Gamma^i - \int_{-\infty}^t \mu(t, s)e^i(t, s)ds.$$

The first terms in the right side of these relationships described the increase of the examined quantities caused by gross investments Γ^i; the second terms reflect the decrease of the corresponding quantities due to the removal of a part of the production equipment from service. If the coefficient of amortisation μ does not depend on time, we obtain from the last equations

$$\frac{dL^i}{dt} = \lambda^i\Gamma^i - \mu L^i, \quad \frac{dE^i}{dt} = \varepsilon^i\Gamma^i - \mu E^i. \tag{4.13}$$

Equations 4.8 and 4.13 are dynamic equations for production factors, while technological coefficients are characteristics of introduced technology. It is easy to see from dynamic equations 4.9 and 4.14, that the technology does not change (technological coefficients are constant), the technological coefficients can be expressed as

$$\lambda^i = \frac{L^i}{K^i}, \quad \varepsilon^i = \frac{E^i}{K^i}.$$

In the case, for example, when

$$\lambda^i < \frac{L^i}{K^i}, \qquad \varepsilon^i < \frac{E^i}{K^i}$$

labour-saving and energy-saving technology is being introduced. We see that it is convenient to introduce dimensionless technological quantities

$$\bar{\lambda}^i = \lambda^i \frac{K^i}{L^i}, \qquad \bar{\varepsilon}^i = \varepsilon^i \frac{K^i}{E^i}$$

which appears to be variables of the set of equation of economic growth.

Note that quantities reciprocal to the technological coefficients are values of equipment which is needed to introduce a unit of labour and a unit of energy in production process or, in other words, prices of introduction of corresponding production factors

$$w^i = \frac{1}{\lambda^i}, \qquad p^i = \frac{1}{\varepsilon^i}. \tag{4.14}$$

If technology does not change, prices of introduction can be written as

$$w^i = \frac{K^i}{L^i}, \qquad p^i = \frac{K^i}{E^i}.$$

So, we can see that price of energy, which one has to take into account, is not a price of energy career, but price of equipment (capital) which allow energy to convert usefully in heat.

4.3 Empirical Estimates of Technological Coefficients

In previous Section, we have obtained equations for dynamics of sectoral production factors which have simple form 4.8 and 4.13, if coefficient of amortisation μ does not depend on time. It is more convenient to proceed further, considering the production system as consisting of the only sector. To introduce technological coefficients for the system, one can sum equations 4.8 and 4.13 to obtain

$$\frac{dK}{dt} = I - \mu K, \qquad \frac{dL}{dt} = \lambda I - \mu L, \qquad \frac{dE}{dt} = \varepsilon I - \mu E. \tag{4.15}$$

Here we define the technological coefficients for the production system as a whole

$$\lambda = \sum_{j=1}^{n} \frac{I^j}{I} \lambda^j, \qquad \varepsilon = \sum_{j=1}^{n} \frac{I^j}{I} \varepsilon^j, \qquad (4.16)$$

where I^j is the gross investment in sector j, and $I = \sum_{j=1}^{n} I^j$ is the gross investment in the whole economy. To characterise technology, it is convenient to use dimensionless technological quantities

$$\bar{\lambda} = \lambda K / L, \qquad \bar{\varepsilon} = \varepsilon K / E.$$

One can use equations 4.15, to estimate technological coefficients $\bar{\lambda}$ and $\bar{\varepsilon}$ as functions of time due to empirical facts. These quantities found on the basis of the time series for the US national economy (see Appendix) are shown in Fig 11.

For a relatively quiet period 1950 – 93, technological coefficients do not change much, so we can estimate mean values

$$\bar{\lambda} = 0.757, \qquad \bar{\varepsilon} = 0.990. \qquad (4.17)$$

Equations 4.15 can be considered as relations which determine a demand of the production factors or real rates of growth which are defined by relations

$$\frac{dK}{dt} = I - \mu K = \delta K, \qquad \frac{dL}{dt} = \lambda I - \mu L = \nu L, \qquad \frac{dE}{dt} = \varepsilon I - \mu E = \eta E.$$
$$(4.18)$$

These equations determine exact relations between real rates of growth of production factors $\delta(t)$, $\nu(t)$, and $\eta(t)$ and technological coefficients

$$\lambda = \frac{\nu + \mu}{\delta + \mu} \frac{L}{K}, \qquad \varepsilon = \frac{\eta + \mu}{\delta + \mu} \frac{E}{K}. \qquad (4.19)$$

The depreciation coefficient μ can be excluded from relations 4.19. So, one can obtain relation between different real rates of growth

$$\delta = \nu + \frac{1 - \bar{\lambda}}{\bar{\varepsilon} - \bar{\lambda}} (\eta - \nu). \qquad (4.20)$$

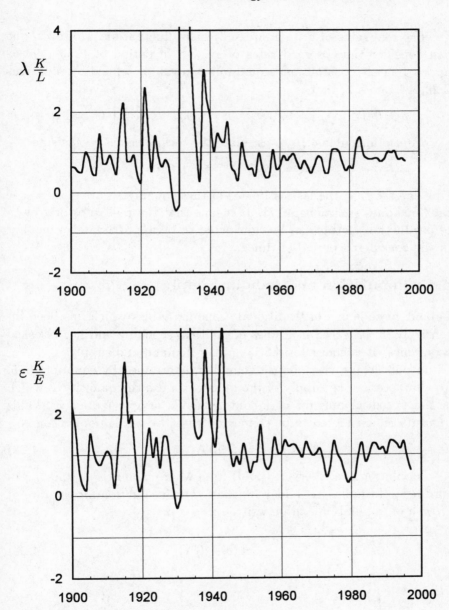

Figure 11 Labour and energy requirements

Values are calculated according to relation 4.15 on the basis of data for the US economy given in Appendix.

The real rates of growth are subject to fluctuation. However, one can consider the observed rates of growth in period of 1950 – 93 as approximately constant and equal to mean values defined by equations 2.20, 4.1 and 4.2, that is,

$$\delta = 0.0427, \quad \nu = 0.0186, \quad \eta = 0.0371, \quad \mu = 0.05. \qquad (4.21)$$

We use formulae 4.19 to estimate the technological coefficients

$$\bar{\lambda} = 0.740, \qquad \bar{\varepsilon} = 0.940.$$

One can see that the last estimates of these quantities are close to the previous ones (relations 4.17). It means that the real rates of growth of production factors can be considered to be approximately constant in the considered period of time.

4.4   Population and Labour Supply

Labour force is one of traditional economic topics which has been intensively investigated in frames of political economy and neo-classical economics. It is characterised by labour demand and supply.

In our theory, the labour demand is determined by equation 4.15. To characterise the supply of the labour, we use the quantity $\tilde{L}$ which is the potential amount of labour available at given price w. This quantity is considered to be connected with the whole population N

$$\tilde{L} = f(w)\, N. \qquad (4.22)$$

Population is a reservoir (pool) from where labour is supplied. According to formulae 1.1 and 1.18, the dynamic equation for the rate of growth of population can be written as

$$\frac{dN}{dt} = (b - d)N, \qquad (4.23)$$

$$b - d = \begin{cases} r - aN, & W = 0 \\ r\,\dfrac{hW/N}{1 + s\,hW/N}, & s = \min \begin{cases} \dfrac{\bar{N}(\infty)}{\bar{N}(\infty) - N} \\ \dfrac{r}{(b-d)_\infty} \end{cases}, & W \neq 0. \end{cases}$$

All quantities in this formula were introduced and estimated in Chapter 1 on the basis of data for the global population growth. Three of these parameters can be considered to be universal, that is, applicable to any nation

$$r \approx 0.0277 \; year^{-1}, \quad a \approx 10^{-6} \; man^{-1} \cdot year^{-1}, \quad h \approx 0.002 \; man \cdot dollar^{-1}.$$
$$(4.24)$$

Asymptotic behaviour of population, that is, the quantity $(b - d)_\infty$ is assumed to be specific and ought to be estimated for every nation considered. However, only developed nations have reached the critical value of national wealth (see Section 1.3).

Apart from population, labour supply depends on the price of labour w, that is, on expenses which are needed to provide a living wage and for training. These expenses are cost of labour. Increasing function $f(w)$ in equation 4.22 changes from zero at $w = 0$ till a certain limiting value which is usually about 0.5 for developed countries.

One can assume that the rate of unemployment

$$u = \frac{\tilde{L} - L}{\tilde{L}}$$

is a decreasing function of the wage $u = u(w)$ or vice versa wage is a decreasing function of unemployment $w = w(u)$. Having considered vast empirical data for different countries, Blanchflower and Oswald (1994) have shown that there exists a universal dependence of wage on unemployment. We slightly modify this function to write it as

$$w(u) = w(0) \left(\frac{\epsilon}{\epsilon + u} \right)^{0.1}, \quad u = \frac{\tilde{L} - L}{\tilde{L}}. \quad (4.25)$$

A small quantity ϵ is installed into the original formula by Blanchflower and Oswald (1994) to avoid infinite value of wage at $u = 0$ which does not practically affect the dependence of wage on unemployment at $\epsilon < 0.01$ and $u > 0.1$. At $\epsilon = 0$, one returns to original formula

$$w(u) = C \, u^{-0.1}, \quad u = (\tilde{L} - L)/\tilde{L},$$

where quantity C is connected with 'further characteristics of the worker and his or her sector' (Blanchflower and Oswald, 1994, p. 5). Equilibrium wage $w(0)$ in equation 4.25 can change from country to country and with time. For the US economy, for example, the quantity can be estimated on the basis of data collected by Blanchflower and Oswald (1994, p. 115)

$$w(0) = 13400\, dollar/man \cdot year, \quad at\ \epsilon = 0.005. \tag{4.26}$$

To obtain an equation for the labour supply, one can differentiate relation 4.22 to get

$$\frac{d\tilde{L}}{dt} = \tilde{\nu}(b - d, w, L, N,)\, \tilde{L},$$

where the potential rate of growth of labour is defined as

$$\tilde{\nu} = \left(b - d - f'(w)\, w'(u)\frac{N}{L}\,(\lambda I - \mu L)\right)\left(1 - f'(w)\, w'(u)\frac{N}{L}\right)^{-1}, \tag{4.27}$$

$$w'(u) = -w(0)\,\frac{0.1}{\epsilon}\left(\frac{\epsilon}{\epsilon + u}\right)^{1.1}, \quad u = \frac{\tilde{L} - L}{\tilde{L}}.$$

The current consumption can be calculated as

$$\Pi = wL, \tag{4.28}$$

where L is the real amount of labour consumption measured in any units, and w is the wage or the price of labour.

4.5 Stock of Knowledge and Energy Supply

To substitute the labour by energy, one ought to have available sources of energy and appliances which allow the use of energy in production aims. Some devices ought to be invented, made and installed for work. Human imagination provides methods of using energy in production aims. So, the base for the energy supply lies in a deposit of knowledge which is fallow, unless it is used in a routine production process. This deposit determines the possibility of the society attracting the extra energy to production. We consider that this stock of knowledge, that is fundamental results of science, results of research, project works and so on (stock of principles of organisation) are products of a sector (sectors) of the production system of the economy and are measured by their value R.[5] This quantity is a governed by an equation from set 2.11, that is

$$\frac{dR}{dt} = H - \mu R, \tag{4.29}$$

where H is a quantitative measure of efforts for creating of principles of organisation per a year, that is, investment in science, research, and developments (but not in education). It is usually a small part of final output

$$H = mY. \tag{4.30}$$

Quantity m is, for example, equal to 0.02 - 0.03 in 1960 – 93 years in the US (Stephan, 1996).

Equation 4.29 determines the structure of stock of knowledge, as well as the structure of stock of production equipment (see Section 2.4), and allow as to calculate value of stock of knowledge R, if investment H is known and rate of depreciation μ of the stock of knowledge can be estimated. Alternatively, stock of knowledge can be measured directly in terms of natural units, that is, by number of patents issued, by number of technical journals, by number of books in print and so on. Can the value of stock of knowledge R be a measure of information which is contained in all this?

Then, activity for materialisation of found possibilities is needed also. Stock of knowledge ought to be considered as a resource itself. Similar to population, stock of knowledge is playing a role of reservoir (pool) (note an analogy of equation 4.29 with equation 1.1) from which applications of energy emerge. One can find plenty of brilliant examples of 'transformation' of knowledge in useful energy in the history of technology. However, little is known about the formal description of this process, so that one can only guess that energy supply $\tilde{E}$ that is,

---

[5]According to Ayres (1997a, p. 35) 'There are two important types of knowledge. One type ("free floating") knowledge concerns the way the world works. It is gained through R&D and can be protected for some time, although it diffuses eventually into books, formulae and designs. ... Free floating knowledge is a "non rival" (i.e. public good). The other type is a private good. It is much more difficult (in fact costly) to transfer. It is gained by learning-by-doing, and by experience. It is embodied in organisations and cultures more than in individuals, although individual skills are also part of this category.'

the amount of energy which can be used in production processes, can be written as a function of two variables

$$\tilde{E} = g(p, R), \tag{4.31}$$

where p is price of introduction of energy in production which can be expressed (see Section 4.2, equation 4.14) as

$$p = \frac{K}{\bar{\varepsilon} E}. \tag{4.32}$$

This estimation that is, the price of attracting the energy, has been appearing on the stage of materialisation of principles of organisation.

To calculate potential rate of energy consumption, equation 4.31 ought to be differentiated which gives

$$\frac{d\tilde{E}}{dt} = \left(\frac{\partial \ln g}{\partial p} \frac{dp}{dt} + \frac{\partial \ln g}{\partial R} \frac{dR}{dt} \right) \tilde{E}.$$

After using equations 4.29 and 4.32, one can write down an equation for energy supply

$$\frac{d\tilde{E}}{dt} = \tilde{\eta}(p, E, R)\tilde{E}, \tag{4.33}$$

where the rate of potential increase of energy can be found from the equation

$$\tilde{\eta} = (H - \mu R) \frac{\partial \ln g}{\partial R} + \left[\left(\frac{1}{\bar{\varepsilon}} - 1 \right) \frac{I}{E} - \frac{d\bar{\varepsilon}}{dt} \frac{K}{\bar{\varepsilon}^2 E} \right] \frac{\partial \ln g}{\partial p}. \tag{4.34}$$

One can see that a rate of potential growth of energy $\tilde{\eta}$ depends on the stock of knowledge R and value of transformation and materialisation of deposited massages p. However, the question is whether function 4.31 really exists. This function remains unknown and, in this situation, potential rate of energy growth ought to be given. The quantities $\tilde{\eta}$ and $\tilde{E}$ are characteristics of the level of technology which is achieved currently.

One can refer to our simple four-sector model of the production system described in Chapter 2 to describe the process of developing of energy supply. Discovering of principle of organisation and developing of projects of technological processes is a content of activity of the third sector. The second sector materialises the projects. One can see that products of the first three sectors are needed to create the means of production for the fourth sector. The last one eventually creates the products man needs.

Of course, there is no question of lack of energy. It is a question of ways of utilisation of energy to get the desired effect. However, we do not know whether the available energy is limited or not. This question is clearly connected with other question: Can the stock of knowledge be limited?

4.6 Investment and Three Modes of Development

Though the potential rates of growth $\tilde{\nu}$ and $\tilde{\eta}$ can be, in principle, calculated as we see in the previous Section, further on, they are assumed to be given. We suppose that the potential rates of growth of production factors are known as functions of time

$$\tilde{\delta} = \tilde{\delta}(t), \qquad \tilde{\nu} = \tilde{\nu}(t), \qquad \tilde{\eta} = \tilde{\eta}(t).$$

In any case the real rates of growth ν and η, defined by equations 4.18, do not exceed the potential rates of growth $\tilde{\nu}$ and $\tilde{\eta}$, that is,

$$\nu \leq \tilde{\nu}, \quad \eta \leq \tilde{\eta}.$$

This determines the restrictions for investments in the production sector

$$I \leq \frac{\mu + \tilde{\nu}}{\lambda} L, \quad I \leq \frac{\mu + \tilde{\eta}}{\varepsilon} E. \tag{4.35}$$

Apart from this, one ought to take into account the restriction imposed by limiting output and necessary level of consumption. It means that investments $I(t)$ are limited, so according to relation 3.59 one can write

$$I \leq Y - wL$$

which implies existence of the potential investment rate of growth $\tilde{\delta}(t)$

$$I \leq (\tilde{\delta} + \mu)K.$$

One can assume that the production system tries to swallow up all available production factors. In this case, the real investments are determined by a competition between potential investments from one side and labour and energy supplies from the other side and one ought to write for investments

$$I = (\delta + \mu)K = \min \begin{cases} (\tilde{\delta} + \mu)K \\ (\tilde{\nu} + \mu)K/\bar{\lambda} \\ (\tilde{\eta} + \mu)K/\bar{\varepsilon} \end{cases} . \tag{4.36}$$

Real rates of growth of production factors δ, ν and η are different from the potential ones. According to three lines of relation 4.36, one can define three modes of economic development for which we have different formulae for calculation. As it is seen from equations 4.18 and 4.36, the real rates of growth can be calculated for three modes as

$$\delta = \tilde{\delta}, \qquad\qquad \nu = (\tilde{\delta} + \mu)\bar{\lambda} - \mu, \qquad \eta = (\tilde{\delta} + \mu)\bar{\varepsilon} - \mu,$$

$$\delta = (\tilde{\nu} + \mu)\frac{1}{\bar{\lambda}} - \mu, \quad \nu = \tilde{\nu}, \qquad\qquad \eta = (\tilde{\nu} + \mu)\frac{\bar{\varepsilon}}{\bar{\lambda}} - \mu,$$

$$\delta = (\tilde{\eta} + \mu)\frac{1}{\bar{\varepsilon}} - \mu, \quad \nu = (\tilde{\eta} + \mu)\frac{\bar{\lambda}}{\bar{\varepsilon}} - \mu, \qquad \eta = \tilde{\eta}.$$

The first set of equations is valid in the case of lack of investment, abundance of labour, energy and raw materials. The second line is valid in the case of lack of labour, abundance of investment, energy and raw materials. The last line of equations is valid in the case of lack of energy, abundance of investment, labour and raw materials.

According to the above speculation, the real rates of growth of production factors are not bigger than the potential ones. It means that gaps between real and potential amounts of production factors, for example, a gap between labour supply $\tilde{L}$ and labour demand L, increase. So, one can see that index of unemployment $u = (\tilde{L} - L)/\tilde{L}$, for example, cannot decrease in the 'natural' way. To decrease the gaps between real and potential amounts of production factors, an intervention in the form of governmental investments is needed, and to take it into account, one can rewrite relation 4.36 in the form

$$I = (\delta + \mu)K = \chi(u)\,K + \min \begin{cases} (\tilde{\delta} + \mu)K \\ (\tilde{\nu} + \mu)K/\bar{\lambda} \\ (\tilde{\eta} + \mu)K/\bar{\varepsilon} \end{cases}. \qquad (4.37)$$

where quantity $\chi(u)$ is designed to regulate the gaps between supply and demand of production factors. In this case, three modes of economic development exist as well.

4.7 Dynamics of Technological Coefficients

To find out the law of the time dependence of the technological coefficients, we refer to the restrictions on investments. According to the three modes defined by relations 4.36, one can obtain three sets of conditions for dimensionless technological quantities $\bar{\lambda}$, $\bar{\varepsilon}$ and their ratio $\Theta = \bar{\varepsilon}/\bar{\lambda}$

$$1 = \frac{\tilde{\delta} + \mu}{\delta + \mu}, \quad \bar{\lambda} \le \frac{\tilde{\nu} + \mu}{\delta + \mu}, \quad \bar{\lambda} \le \frac{\tilde{\nu} + \mu}{\tilde{\delta} + \mu}, \quad \bar{\varepsilon} \le \frac{\tilde{\eta} + \mu}{\delta + \mu}, \quad \bar{\varepsilon} \le \frac{\tilde{\eta} + \mu}{\tilde{\delta} + \mu},$$

$$1 \le \frac{\tilde{\delta} + \mu}{\delta + \mu}, \quad \bar{\lambda} = \frac{\tilde{\nu} + \mu}{\delta + \mu}, \quad \bar{\lambda} \ge \frac{\tilde{\nu} + \mu}{\tilde{\delta} + \mu}, \quad \bar{\varepsilon} \le \frac{\tilde{\eta} + \mu}{\delta + \mu}, \quad \Theta \le \frac{\tilde{\eta} + \mu}{\tilde{\nu} + \mu},$$

$$1 \le \frac{\tilde{\delta} + \mu}{\delta + \mu}, \quad \bar{\lambda} \le \frac{\tilde{\nu} + \mu}{\delta + \mu}, \quad \bar{\varepsilon} = \frac{\tilde{\eta} + \mu}{\delta + \mu}, \quad \bar{\varepsilon} \ge \frac{\tilde{\eta} + \mu}{\tilde{\delta} + \mu}, \quad \Theta \ge \frac{\tilde{\eta} + \mu}{\tilde{\nu} + \mu}.$$

$$(4.38)$$

In the last two of the three modes, one of the production factors is limited. In the first case, there is an internal restriction to growth.

One can assume that there are internal technological changes which lead to changes of technological coefficients, whereas the economic system tries to use all available resources. It means that the technological coefficients have tendencies to change in such a way that the inequalities in conditions 4.38 are moving towards the equalities. These processes are connected with the propagation of known technologies. One can consider rates of growth

$$\frac{d\Theta}{dt}, \quad \frac{d\bar{\lambda}}{dt}, \quad \frac{d\bar{\varepsilon}}{dt}$$

to be functions of differences

$$\Theta - \frac{\tilde{\eta} + \mu}{\tilde{\nu} + \mu}, \quad \bar{\lambda} - \frac{\tilde{\nu} + \mu}{\tilde{\delta} + \mu}, \quad \bar{\varepsilon} - \frac{\tilde{\eta} + \mu}{\tilde{\delta} + \mu}.$$

These tendencies of technological changes in the first approximation can be described by equations for dimensionless quantities

$$\frac{d\Theta}{dt} = -\frac{1}{\tau_\theta}\left(\Theta - \frac{\tilde{\eta} + \mu}{\tilde{\nu} + \mu}\right), \tag{4.39}$$

$$\frac{d\bar{\lambda}}{dt} = -\frac{1}{\tau_\lambda}\left(\bar{\lambda} - \frac{\tilde{\nu} + \mu}{\tilde{\delta} + \mu}\right), \tag{4.40}$$

$$\frac{d\bar{\varepsilon}}{dt} = -\frac{1}{\tau_\varepsilon}\left(\bar{\varepsilon} - \frac{\tilde{\eta} + \mu}{\tilde{\delta} + \mu}\right). \tag{4.41}$$

So as $\Theta = \bar{\varepsilon}/\bar{\lambda}$, only two of equations 4.39 – 4.41 are independent. For equations 4.39, 4.40, and 4.41 to be consistent, relaxation times τ_λ and τ_ε ought to be equated and to be connected with relaxation time τ_θ that is,

$$\tau_\lambda = \tau_\varepsilon = \frac{1}{\bar{\lambda}}\frac{\tilde{\nu} + \mu}{\tilde{\delta} + \mu}\,\tau_\theta.$$

Equations 4.39 – 4.41 are the first-order approximations to relaxation equations with respect to the quantities written there in brackets, so that one ought to take the zero-order terms of the relaxation times in these equations. It means that in the considered approximation, all relaxation times are equal to each other, namely,

$$\tau_\lambda = \tau_\varepsilon = \tau_\theta = \tau, \tag{4.42}$$

so that subscripts in equations 4.39 – 4.41 can be omitted in the following exposition.

It is easy to see that, if the rates of growth are constant, equation 4.39, for example, at initial value

$$\Theta(0) = (1 - \Delta)\frac{\tilde{\eta} + \mu}{\tilde{\nu} + \mu}$$

has a simple solution

$$\Theta(t) = \frac{\tilde{\eta} + \mu}{\tilde{\nu} + \mu}\left[1 - \Delta \exp\left(-\frac{t}{\tau}\right)\right]. \qquad (4.43)$$

So, the meaning of τ is time of crossover from one technological situation to another, when external parameters $\tilde{\nu}$ and $\tilde{\eta}$ change. It is determined by internal processes of attracting of the proper technology.

4.8 Technological Coefficients and Mechanism of Evolution of Production System

Now we return to the microeconomic approach and consider the production system to consist of numerous enterprises, each of them including one or more *technological processes* as was discussed in Section 3.6. The latter are considered as *atoms* of the production system. Each technological process consumes some products to output other ones. In other words, the enterprise transforms the input set of products $x_j, x_i, \ldots$, where labels of products $j, i, \ldots$ are fixed, into an output set: $x_l, x_m, \ldots$, where labels of products $l, m, \ldots$ are also fixed. It is convenient to use the input and output vectors u and v with non-negative components u_k and v_k, $k = 1, 2, \ldots, n$. This side of technological process was considered in Section 3.6.

Apart from it, each technological process is characterised by equipment costing K and the production factors labour L and energy E needed to animate the production equipment. So, the technological process or the enterprise can be given by a set of five quantities

$$\text{u, v, } K, L, E$$

or, considering the scale of production to be non-essential, by four quantities

$$\frac{\text{u}}{K}, \frac{\text{v}}{K}, r_1 = \frac{L}{K}, r_2 = \frac{E}{K}. \qquad (4.44)$$

The technological process can be depicted by a point in a many-dimensional space which consists of input-output space (Fig. 9) and production-factor space (Fig. 12).

According to Schumpeter (1911), mechanism of evolution of the production system can be imagined as emergence, growth and disappearing of technological processes. An essential moment in this scheme is emergence of a new enterprise, which can use a known technology or create a new one. In the first case one says about diffusion of the known technology. The values of quantities 4.44 are the same for all enterprises with similar technology. One says that the production expands extensively. In the second case new technological processes appear. The new enterprise (technological process) produces either known products by new methods (process innovation), or quite new products (product innovation). In any case the values of quantities 4.44 arise in new combinations. Investigating of new combinations of production factors and setting up a new technological process is not a simple business. Some people take the risk to run such businesses. According to Schumpeter (1911), a new-enterpreneur is a central figure of economic development.

We do not discuss stages of infancy, adolescence, maturity and senescence which can be found in an other place (Ayres, 1997a, p.23). For simplicity, we assume that a technological process remains unchanged until moment of disappearing and consider elementary acts of evolution of production system to be emergence and reproduction of a new technological process. One can enumerate all technological processes according to the time of their emergence by a label α ($\alpha = 1, 2, \ldots$). An enterprise (technological process) with characteristics K^α, L^α, E^α emerges at moment t^α and disappears at moment $t^\alpha + \tau$. For simplicity, the time of existence of the enterprises τ is assumed to be equal for all enterprises. The quantities K^α, L^α, E^α and t^α are random ones, so *an emergence distribution function* ought to be introduced. It is convenient to use variables t^α, r_1^α, r_2^α ($\alpha = 1, 2, \ldots$) as arguments of the emergency function.

Now, one can define sense of technological progress in terms of microeconomical variables r_1 and r_2. Empirical data for what we believed to be a progressively developing US economy (formulae 2.17, 4.1 and 4.2) shows that the rate of capital growth exceeds the rates of growth of

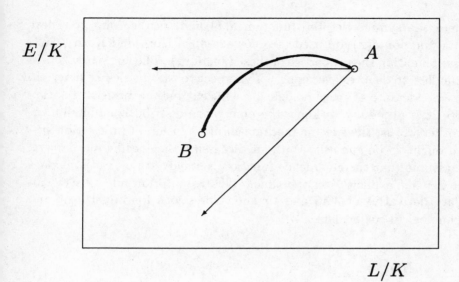

Figure 12 Space of production factors

The area inside the sector is an area of more effective technologies.

---

labour and energy, whereas the rate of energy growth exceeds the rate of labour growth; so an for enterprise to participate in a technological progress the relations between the variables ought to be

$$r_1^\alpha < r_1^0, \quad r_2^\alpha < r_2^0, \quad r_2^\alpha/r_1^\alpha > r_2^0/r_1^0, \tag{4.45}$$

where the zero suffix denotes values of quantities of the foregoing (initial) technology. It can be seen in Fig. 12 that a point corresponding to a progressively new technology falls in a sector of more productive technologies.

Then, expression for production factors can be defined. One can neglect deterioration of the equipment and write down

$$K(t) = \sum_\alpha \langle K^\alpha \left[\theta(t - t^\alpha) - \theta(t - \tau - t^\alpha) \right] \rangle,$$

$$L(t) = \sum_\alpha \langle L^\alpha \left[\theta(t - t^\alpha) - \theta(t - \tau - t^\alpha) \right] \rangle,$$

$$E(t) = \sum_\alpha \langle E^\alpha \left[\theta(t - t^\alpha) - \theta(t - \tau - t^\alpha) \right] \rangle, \tag{4.46}$$

where the symmetric step function $\theta(x)$ and, further on, the Dirac delta-function $\delta(x)$ are used (see, for example, Korn and Korn (1968) for explanation the properties of these functions). The angle brackets in formula 4.46 denotes averaging with respect to the emergence function.

To calculate the technological coefficient on the basis of relation 4.46, it is necessary to know the emergence distribution function or, in other words, the specific mechanism of evolution of production system ought to be guessed. Without discussing the specific mechanism, we assume that the emergence function is steady-state that is, it does not depend explicitly on the time. This assumption allow us to calculate derivative of 4.46 and to find expressions for investment and technological coefficients

$$I(t) = \sum_{\alpha} \langle K^{\alpha} \left[\delta(t - t^{\alpha}) - \delta(t - \tau - t^{\alpha}) \right] \rangle,$$

$$\lambda(t) = \frac{1}{I(t)} \sum_{\alpha} \langle r_1^{\alpha} K^{\alpha} \left[\delta(t - t^{\alpha}) - \delta(t - \tau - t^{\alpha}) \right] \rangle,$$

$$\varepsilon(t) = \frac{1}{I(t)} \sum_{\alpha} \langle r_2^{\alpha} K^{\alpha} \left[\delta(t - t^{\alpha}) - \delta(t - \tau - t^{\alpha}) \right] \rangle. \qquad (4.47)$$

Time dependence of technological coefficients is determined by dependence of variables r_1 and r_2 on index α. To estimate behaviour of technological coefficients, one can introduce two dimentionless functions of the index and represent

$$r_1^{\alpha} = r_1^0 (1 - \varphi_1(\alpha)), \quad r_2^{\alpha} = r_2^0 (1 - \varphi_2(\alpha)), \quad \varphi_1(\alpha) > \varphi_2(\alpha). \qquad (4.48)$$

In accordance with relations 4.45, $\varphi_1(\alpha)$ and $\varphi_2(\alpha)$ are small positive quantities in the case of progressive evolution of production system.

It allows one to see an obvious result: the technological coefficients are diminishing functions of time in this case. This approach allows one to investigate details of the mechanism of evolution of the production system.

4.9 Technological Coefficients and Technological Matrices

To characterise technology, the fundamental technological matrices A and B were introduced in Section 3.1 and technological coefficients λ and ε in Section 4.2. One can guess that these quantities are connected with each other. At least, we can try to establish some relations in the frame of the multi-sector model of the economy which was described in Chapter 3. However, the values of the technological coefficients are determined by level of development of science, and of technological research. So, we ought to determine the technological coefficients as function of some variables which characterise the development of science and technology.

Production equipment produced in sector j are characterised by primary technological coefficients λ_j and ε_j. The basic production equipment of sector j is a mixture of products with different technological coefficients

$$\lambda^j = \sum_{i=1}^{n} \frac{I_i^j}{I^j} \lambda_i, \qquad \varepsilon^j = \sum_{i=1}^{n} \frac{I_i^j}{I^j} \varepsilon_i, \qquad I^j = \sum_{i=1}^{n} I_i^j, \qquad (4.49)$$

where I_i^j is the gross investment of product i in sector j.

The last relations can be written in another form. First of all, we transform one of equations 4.49 in following way, summing up

$$\sum_{i=1}^{n} \lambda^i I^i = \sum_{l=1}^{n} \lambda_l I_l.$$

Then we use formulae 3.15 for investment I_l, which gives

$$\sum_{i=1}^{n} \lambda^i I^i = \sum_{i,l=1}^{n} \bar{b}_l^i \lambda_l I^i$$

and in virtue of the arbitrary values of the sectoral investments I^i, we have for technological coefficients

$$\lambda^j = \sum_{i=1}^{n} \bar{b}_i^j \lambda_i, \qquad \varepsilon^j = \sum_{i=1}^{n} \bar{b}_i^j \varepsilon_i. \qquad (4.50)$$

It is clear that the primary technological coefficients λ_i and ε_i depend only on the amount of products used in production. So,

$$\lambda_i = \lambda_i(X_1^i, X_2^i, \ldots, X_n^i),$$

$$\varepsilon_i = \varepsilon_i(X_1^i, X_2^i, \ldots, X_n^i).$$

One can assume that technological coefficients do not depend on scale of production, so one can consider technological coefficients to be uniform functions of the zeroth power, that is, their arguments have to be grouped in ratios. If we consider a simple case, when equation 3.3 is valid as an approximation at slow changes of technology, the technological coefficients can be written as a function of components of technological matrix A.

$$\lambda_i = \lambda_i(a_1^i, a_2^i, \ldots, a_n^i), \qquad (4.51)$$

$$\varepsilon_i = \varepsilon_i(a_1^i, a_2^i, \ldots, a_n^i),$$

where i is the label of the sectors which output production equipment. In the general case, one has to keep dependence of the primary technological coefficients on the quantities X_j^i, $(i, j = 1, 2, \ldots n)$ which can be evaluated from equations 3.1.

So, one can write down for sectoral technological coefficients

$$\lambda^j = \sum_{i=1}^{n} \bar{b}_i^j \lambda_i(a_1^i, a_2^i, \ldots, a_n^i), \qquad (4.52)$$

$$\varepsilon^j = \sum_{i=1}^{n} \bar{b}_i^j \varepsilon_i(a_1^i, a_2^i, \ldots, a_n^i).$$

The technological coefficients are determined as functions of the components of fundamental technological matrices A and B which are considered to depend on time (see section 3.1). However, in contrast to formula 4.50, results 4.52 are not exact: we refer to relation 3.3 instead 3.1. Moreover, dependence 4.52 ought to be approximated from empirical data, and one can see that possible approximation depends on our choice of sectors. The number of sectors we ought to take into account must be rather large to reflect technological changes. Otherwise, it appears to be insufficient to describe the characteristics of technological changes: intrasectoral technological changes are possible. In contrast to it, the technological coefficients appear to be invariant measures of technological changes. These quantities are very sensitive to technological changes and can be easily estimated on empirical data. So, the technological coefficients are good as fundamental characteristics of technological changes.

We can illustrate these general relations by our simple example of four-sector production system, in which only one sector produces production equipment with technological coefficients λ_2 and ε_2. In this simple case, all basic equipment in all sectors is the product of the second sector. So,

$$\lambda^1 = \lambda^2 = \lambda^3 = \lambda^4 = \lambda_2, \quad \varepsilon^1 = \varepsilon^2 = \varepsilon^3 = \varepsilon^4 = \varepsilon_2.$$

According to expression 4.52, the technological coefficients can be written as a function of components of technological matrix $\mathbf{A}$

$$\lambda_2 = \lambda_2(a_1^2, a_2^2, a_3^2), \qquad \varepsilon_2 = \varepsilon_2(a_1^2, a_2^2, a_3^2).$$

One can believe that the increase of product of science, research, and development ensures technological progress, so dependence can be approximated in a simple way

$$\lambda_2 \sim \left(\frac{a_3^2}{a_1^2 + a_2^2} \right)^{-v}, \qquad \varepsilon_2 \sim \left(\frac{a_3^2}{a_1^2 + a_2^2} \right)^{-u}.$$

It gives decrease of coefficients λ_1 and ε_1 at positive values of indexes v and u.

4.10   Trajectories of Evolution

To consider evolution of the production factors, we collect in this Section the main equations of this Chapter.

The rates of growth of the production factors are defined by equations 4.15, that is,

$$\frac{dK}{dt} = (i - \mu)K, \quad \frac{dL}{dt} = (\bar{\lambda}\, i - \mu)\, L, \quad \frac{dE}{dt} = (\bar{\varepsilon}\, i - \mu)\, E, \quad (4.53)$$

where $i = I/K$. The technological variables $\bar{\lambda}$ and $\bar{\varepsilon}$ characterise a level of applied technology and are determined by equations 4.40 and 4.41, that is,

$$\frac{d\bar{\lambda}}{dt} = -\frac{1}{\tau}\left(\bar{\lambda} - \frac{\tilde{\nu} + \mu}{\tilde{\delta} + \mu}\right), \quad \frac{d\bar{\varepsilon}}{dt} = -\frac{1}{\tau}\left(\bar{\varepsilon} - \frac{\tilde{\eta} + \mu}{\tilde{\delta} + \mu}\right), \qquad (4.54)$$

where τ is time of crossover from one technological situation to another. It is determined by internal processes of developing technology.

These relationship ought to be completed by definition of investments 4.36, that is,

$$i = \min \begin{cases} (\tilde{\delta} + \mu) \\ (\tilde{\nu} + \mu)/\bar{\lambda} \\ (\tilde{\eta} + \mu)/\bar{\varepsilon} \end{cases} . \qquad (4.55)$$

The potential rates of growth $\tilde{\nu}(t)$ and $\tilde{\eta}(t)$ are exogenous characteristics which are considered to be functions of time. The potential rate of growth of investment $\tilde{\delta}$ is an inherent characteristic of production system and it cannot be given arbitrarily. It is determined by internal restriction due to relation between output, investment and consumption

$$Y = I + wL.$$

So, in any case, the potential rate of growth of investment is restricted by inequalities

$$-\mu < \tilde{\delta} < \frac{Y}{K} - \mu. \qquad (4.56)$$

The potential rate of growth of investment $\tilde{\delta}$ can also be determined through potential sectoral investments $\tilde{I}^j$ which were discussed in Section 3.5

$$\tilde{\delta} = -\mu + \frac{1}{K}\sum_{i=1}^{n}\tilde{I}^i. \qquad (4.57)$$

A simple relation between the real rates of growth – equation 4.20 – exists. One can assume that there is a preferred relation between the

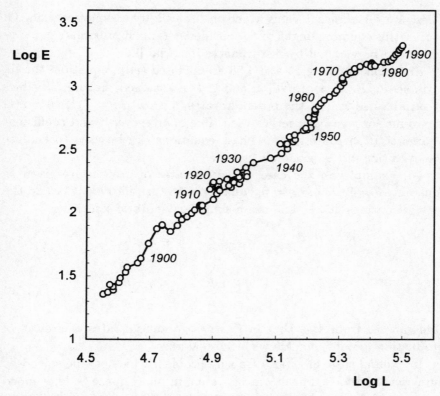

Figure 13 The real trajectory of development

The curve reflects drastic events in the US economy: the crisis of the late twenties – beginning of the thirties and the energy crisis of the beginning of the eighties.

---

potential rates of growth as well. So, the potential rate of growth of investment $\tilde{\delta}$ tends to the quantity

$$\tilde{\nu} + \frac{1 - \bar{\lambda}}{\bar{\varepsilon} - \bar{\lambda}} \, (\tilde{\eta} - \tilde{\nu}).$$

An arbitrary potential rate of capital growth approaches this value according, for example, to the law

$$\frac{d\tilde{\delta}}{dt} = -\frac{1}{\tau} \left(\tilde{\delta} - \tilde{\nu} - \frac{1 - \bar{\lambda}}{\bar{\varepsilon} - \bar{\lambda}} \, (\tilde{\eta} - \tilde{\nu}) \right). \tag{4.58}$$

There are social mechanisms which ensure validity of equation 4.58. Of course, this equation ought to be considered as an approximate equality which can be violated by disturbances in social life.

Equations 4.53 – 4.55 and 4.58 are a closed set of equations for six variables L, E, K, $i = I/K$, $\bar{\lambda}$, and $\bar{\varepsilon}$. It is assumed that initial values of variables as well as the potential rates of growth $\tilde{\nu} = \tilde{\nu}(t)$, $\tilde{\eta} = \tilde{\eta}(t)$ of production factors together with time of crossover τ and coefficient of amortisation μ are given. These equations can be used to analyse the evolution of the economic system.

For example, in the case, when all rates of growth are given as constant: $\delta = \tilde{\delta}$, $\nu = \tilde{\nu}$, $\eta = \tilde{\eta}$, equation 4.58 turn into identity and the set of equations 4.53 – 4.55 has a simple asymptotic solution

$$K = K_0 e^{\delta t}, \quad L = L_0 e^{\nu t}, \quad E = E_0 e^{\eta t},$$

$$i = \delta + \mu, \quad \bar{\lambda} = \frac{\nu + \mu}{\delta + \mu}, \quad \bar{\varepsilon} = \frac{\eta + \mu}{\delta + \mu}. \tag{4.59}$$

One can see from 4.59 that in this case potential rates of growth of production factors coincide with the real ones.

In general case, one has a Cauchy problem which can be solved by numerical methods. Movement of system in phase space is determined by external potential rates of growth of labour and energy $\tilde{\nu}$ and $\tilde{\eta}$. One can see from the example of real trajectory shown in Fig. 13 that the movement can be rather complex.

5 Mechanism of Estimation of Value

In previous chapters, the price as an empirical estimates of the value of the product was used. It was noted that the price is not an intrinsic characteristic of the product but a result of human being estimation. A mechanism of estimation was discovered in frame of classical political economy (Maltus, 1798; Say, 1803) and, especially, of neo-classical economics (Marshall, 1920; Walras, 1874; Hicks, 1946). The prices are estimated from two sides: *a producer* estimates the efforts needed to create the thing, *a consumer* estimates value of the thing according to its usefulness for him (Marshall, 1920). Price is a result of agreement between the producer and the consumer. The prices appear to be connected with peculiarities of behaviour of the producers and the consumers. However, it does not mean that the price is a quite subjective quantity. The price is more than cost of production by the amount the consumer can willingly pay. Relationship between producers and consumers in the process of exchange of products is a market of products. Theory of prices is a theory of the market.

To consider mechanism of estimation of value, one needs to introduce an heuristic model of the society which in the simplest case can be imagined as consisting of many independent economic subjects and government as the central economic subject who presumably represents the common interest (external and internal security, infrastructure, social programs, environment and so on) of all members of the society. Though activity of the government as economic subject is very important to keep the economic system in action, one can start, following Walras (1874), with discussion of fully disintegrated system – a set of independent individual subjects. This main idea about interaction between producers and consumers was elaborated quantitatively for many special cases (Baumol, 1977). In this chapter, we consider the theory of prices for a simple scheme, which can be described in macroeconomic terms.

5.1   Economic Subjects

In the basis of economic activity of human beings, one can find explicit or implicit wishes to satisfy the necessities of life. In human society, each member needs the services of other persons which he receives in exchange of his services to other members. So, one can assert that the essential content of economic activity of human being is exchange of the services. This is a main thing which unites human beings in society. 'Every man thus lives by exchanging or becomes in some measure a merchant, and the society itself grows to be what is properly a commercial society' (Smith, 1776, Ch. 4). The exchange of the services has the form of exchange of products.

An economic agent (subject) as a carrier of will and a source of decisions on the operation of exchange has been appearing in the theory. Strictly speaking, each member of the society is an economic subject (agent). It is assumed that the subject knows what is good and what is bad for him, in other words, he has a certain *system of values*, which can be different for different subjects, though some values can be mutual ones. Each economic subject tries to improve his situation, however beautiful it is.

Every economic agent acts as *a producer* and *a consumer* simultaneously. As a producer he spends some effort of different kinds $\hat{e}_1, \hat{e}_2, \ldots, \hat{e}_m$ to create products. As a consumer he uses a set of products $\check{x}_1, \check{x}_2, \ldots, \check{x}_n$. One can assume that every agent tries to spend less effort to get more products. To describe the behaviour of the economic agent and his tendency to improve his situation, one introduces characteristics of the economic agent, namely, a utility function

$$u(\hat{e}, \check{x}) = u(\hat{e}_1, \hat{e}_2, \ldots, \hat{e}_m, \ \check{x}_1, \check{x}_2, \ldots, \check{x}_n) \tag{5.1}$$

which is decreasing function in co-ordinates $\hat{e}_1, \hat{e}_2, \ldots, \hat{e}_m$ and increasing function in co-ordinates $\check{x}_1, \check{x}_2, \ldots, \check{x}_n$. In the next Section, we will start with preferences of an agent to determine the agent's subjective utility function formally.

As a producer, the economic agent tries to decrease in his efforts and, as a consumer, he tries to increase in amount of products he can obtain for the efforts, so that, speaking formally, the agent tries to reach the greatest value of this function at some restriction. If one considers a single economic agent, the restriction can be written in the form

$$\sum_{i=1}^{n} p_i \check{x}_i \leq \sum_{j=1}^{m} w_j \hat{e}_j, \tag{5.2}$$

where p_i is a price of product number i, w_j is a money estimate of a unit of effort of kind j. Restriction 5.2 means that the agent cannot spend more than he or she gets. Some other restrictions ought to be taken into account as well. To construct the proper theory, one has to consider all the economic subjects simultaneously.

In modern societies, a separate person can be considered as a consumer, but finished products are usually created by enterprises which ought to be considered as economic agents themselves. As a producer, an enterprise unites some technological processes, attracts a great deal of production factors and acts as was described in Sections 3.6 and 4.8. The behaviour of the enterprise is determined by tendency to get the greatest profit at given prices p_i and w_j, that is, speaking formally, the aim of the enterprise is to maximise an object function

$$\pi(\check{e}, \hat{x}) = \sum_{i=1}^{n} p_i \hat{x}_i - \sum_{j=1}^{m} w_j \check{e}_j \geq 0. \tag{5.3}$$

It means that the enterprise tries to increase in the output $\hat{x}_1, \hat{x}_2, \ldots, \hat{x}_n$ and decrease in the consumed efforts $\check{e}_1, \check{e}_2, \ldots, \check{e}_m$.

According to Walras (1874), the economic system can be imagined as consisting of many, say, S consumers and P producers, everyone of them independently running business according their rules, but, nevertheless, they depend on each other through exchange of efforts and products. Every consumer ($\alpha = 1, 2, \ldots, S$) is characterised by the effort supply $\hat{e}^{\alpha}$ and the product demand $\check{x}^{\alpha}$ which are arguments of the utility function of the kind of 5.1. Every producer ($\gamma = 1, 2, \ldots, P$) is characterised by the effort demand $\check{e}^{\gamma}$ and the product supply $\hat{x}^{\gamma}$ which are arguments of the profit function of the kind of 5.3. To determine the efforts and the products, one ought to find maximum of S utility functions of the type 5.1 and P profit functions of the type 5.3, taking restrictions due to balance relations for efforts, products, and profits into account.

Walras (1874) succeeded in writing down a set of equations for all the variables which appear to be equations for the prices and wages as well. Later, Wald (1951), Arrow and Debreu (1954) and McKenzie (1959) have shown that the set of equations has a non-negative solution which confirms adequacy of the theory for this case. The proof required powerful and esoteric mathematical tools which fascinated a few generations of mathematical economists who have written thousands of papers.[1] So, it was shown that the proposed mechanism of exchanges can be taken as a basis for explanation of mechanism of human estimation of prices and, consequently, of value of any set of products.

The theory refers to principles of behaviour of economic agents which, in general form, are universal, they are valid whichever economic system, capitalism or socialism is realised. These formal principles are laid in the foundation of the theory of exchange, or the theory of market. Simultaneously, it is a theory of prices. Though some general principles of behaviour of the producers and consumers appear to be universal, the theory of market in such system depends apparently on the assumptions about amount of participants of each kind and their possible alliances, that is, about architecture of the system which can be rather complicated and cannot be universal. The economic system has been investigated at different assumptions (Baumol, 1977).

5.2   Subjective Utility Function

It was shown (von Neumann and Morgenstern, 1953) that one can start with human preferences to define utility function. Formalisation of man's preferences leads to a subjective utility function which is a characteristics of an economic subject.

Let us consider a fixed set of products, which can be considered as a vector

$$\mathsf{x} = \left\| \begin{array}{c} x_1 \\ \cdot \\ \cdot \\ \cdot \\ x_n \end{array} \right\|. \tag{5.4}$$

---

[1]Mark Blaug (1998, p. 17) evaluates that 'The result of all this is that we now understand almost less of how actual markets work than did Adam Smith or even Léon Walras.'

The first candidate for the function which can characterise the given amount of products in their relation to human being's needs, is the value of these products. But one must decline this candidate on the basis we have discussed in Chapter 1: the value of a set of a product appears to be not a function of amounts of products at all (see Section 1.2). Instead of value function, one uses utility function, which is introduced here in the following way.

To compare two sets of products, that is, vectors x^1 and x^2, one introduces the relations between vectors. Man can estimate whether he prefers the set x^1 to the set x^2, or, on the contrary, the set x^2 to the set x^1, or he cannot distinguish between two sets, correspondingly:

$$x^1 \succ x^2, \quad x^2 \succ x^1, \quad x^1 \sim x^2.$$

It was shown (von Neumann and Morgenstern, 1953) that monotonically increasing function on space R_n can be defined, such that

$$x^1 \succ x^2 \Rightarrow u(x^1) > u(x^2), \tag{5.5}$$

$$x^1 \sim x^2 \Rightarrow u(x^1) = u(x^2).$$

The arrow $\Rightarrow$ shows that the right-hand-side relation follows the left-hand-side one.

If an amount of at least one separate product in the set x^1 is more than the amount of the same product in the set x^2, then

$$x^1 \succ x^2 \Rightarrow u(x^1) > u(x^2).$$

It means that all partial derivatives of the function are positive

$$\frac{\partial u}{\partial x_j} > 0. \tag{5.6}$$

Then, it is assumed that the mixture of two sets x^1 and x^2 is preferred to any of the sets, consequently

$$u(\lambda x^1 + (1 - \lambda)x^2) > u(x^1),$$

$$u(\lambda x^1 + (1 - \lambda)x^2) > u(x^2), \quad 0 < \lambda < 1.$$

It is followed by a relation

$$u(\lambda x^1 + (1 - \lambda)x^2) > \lambda u(x^1) + (1 - \lambda)u(x^2).$$

It means that function u is strictly convex and a matrix of second partial derivatives

$$u_{ij} = \frac{\partial^2 u}{\partial x_i \partial x_j} \tag{5.7}$$

that is, the Hesse matrix is negatively determined.

The above described function $u(x_1, x_2, \ldots, x_n)$ is called a utility function, exactly, a subjective utility function. The properties of the utility function are determined by postulates which are reflection of empirical evidence. One can note that any monotonically increasing transformation of variables of the utility function determines a new utility function with the same properties. These function ought to be considered to be identical.

5.3   Demand Functions

Now, we shall consider a separate consumer who owns some amount of money and can decide what products are the most necessary ones for him. We can think that this consumer has some income M which is obtained in exchange for his efforts e_i, while label i $(i = 1, 2, \ldots, m)$ enumerates kinds of efforts. This income has a money form and it increases, when the agent's efforts increase, so in the simplest case one can write down

$$M = \sum_{i=1}^{m} w_i \, e_i, \tag{5.8}$$

where w_i is a money estimate of a unit of effort of kind i.

Then, the money is spent for acquiring products according to consumers preferences. One believes that the main thing is to get money, if it is got, there is no difficulty to acquire any thing. This assertion can be formalised in theory (Walras, 1874) as

$$p_1 x_1 + p_2 x_2 + \ldots + p_n x_n \leq M, \tag{5.9}$$

where p_i is a price of product, x_i is quantity of acquiring products. It was supposed here that there are no other restriction. It is not always true. In certain societies there is another mechanism of distribution of products. In centrally planned societies, existence of money does not mean that a person can buy any products. It is necessary to have a special right to buy the products. This right is reached by increase in social rank of the person, so the main aim of person's activity is to increase social rank (Voslenskii, 1984). It is not surprisingly that 'scientific norms of consumption' were elaborated in such societies.

Then, we assume that the consumer is characterised by a subjective utility function

$$u(x_1, x_2, \ldots, x_n),$$

where x_1, x_2,...,x_n are amounts of products.

One assumes that in any circumstances the consumer chooses such a set of products that utility function would have the biggest value, that is, one can describe consumer's behaviour as a way of maximisation of the utility function

$$\max u(x_1, x_2, \ldots, x_n)$$

with restriction 5.9. Amount of money M for acquiring of the desirable set of products is given, as well as prices p_i of all products. One can notice that budget restriction 5.9 can written in form of equality, so, the problem of choice can be solved as problem of conditional maximisation

$$\max u(x_1, x_2, \ldots, x_n), \quad \sum_{i=1}^{n} p_i x_i = M, \quad \mathsf{x} \geq 0. \qquad (5.10)$$

There are no difficulties in adding some other restrictions to the problem, if they exist.

To solve the problem, one starts with the Lagrange function

$$\mathcal{L}(\mathsf{x}, \lambda) = u(\mathsf{x}) - \lambda \left(\sum_{i=1}^{n} p_i x_i - M \right),$$

where λ is a Lagrange multiplier. One ought to equate partial derivatives of Lagrange function to zero to obtain a set of equations for unknown quantities

$$\frac{\partial u}{\partial x_j} - \lambda p_j = 0, \qquad (5.11)$$

$$M - \sum_{i=1}^{n} p_i x_i = 0. \qquad (5.12)$$

The first of the equations defines the ratio of product prices as a ratio of the marginal utilities of the products, that is, as a ratio of the first derivatives of utility function

$$\frac{\partial u}{\partial x_i} : \frac{\partial u}{\partial x_j} = \frac{p_i}{p_j}, \qquad i, j = 1, 2, \dots, n. \tag{5.13}$$

These relations were written by Marshall (1920, Mathematical Appendix II).

Solution of equations 5.11 and 5.12 can be written in the form of functions of the quantities x_i and λ on the parameters of the problem

$$x_i = x_i(\mathsf{p}, M), \quad \lambda = \lambda(\mathsf{p}, M). \tag{5.14}$$

The solution of the problem gives rise to a demand function, which itself can be laid in the foundation of the theory. In fact, one ought to assume special properties of utility function for functions 5.14 would describe the empirical facts.

A change of scale of value does not change the problem, so that one can define a demand function as uniform function of its arguments, that is,

$$x_i = x_i \left(\frac{\mathsf{p}}{M} \right). \tag{5.15}$$

Effects of prices and money on demand can be investigated without knowing utility function in explicit form (Slutzki, 1915; Hicks, 1946).

If the utility function is given, the demand functions can be found easily. For example, for utility function

$$u = x_1^{\alpha_1} x_2^{\alpha_2} \cdots x_n^{\alpha_n}, \quad \sum_{i=1}^{n} \alpha_i < 1$$

a solution to problem 5.10 is

$$x_i(\mathsf{p}, M) = \frac{\alpha_i M}{\alpha p_i}, \quad \lambda(\mathsf{p}, M) = \alpha \frac{u}{M}, \quad \alpha = \sum_{i=1}^{n} \alpha_i. \tag{5.16}$$

However, the demand function can be determined from empirical data independently. The demand functions are usually decreasing functions of prices, though there are some exceptions to this rule.

5.4 Welfare Function

The utility function, considered in Section 5.2, is based on the consumer's subjective preferences and can be called *a subjective utility function*. It can be introduced for each consumer, who tries to choose a situation to maximise this function. To investigate links between these utility functions and the objective utility function considered in Section 1.2, one has to introduce the subjective utility function for the whole community.

Consider a society consisting of S independent consumers which hold together some amount of products

$$Q_1, Q_2, \ldots, Q_n,$$

while consumer α owns parts of the products

$$x_1^\alpha, x_2^\alpha, \ldots, x_n^\alpha, \quad \alpha = 1, 2, \ldots, S,$$

whereas

$$\sum_{\alpha=1}^{S} x_i^\alpha = Q_i, \quad i = 1, 2, \ldots, n. \tag{5.17}$$

One assumes that consumer's utility function

$$u^\alpha(\mathsf{x}^1, \mathsf{x}^2, \ldots, \mathsf{x}^S), \quad \alpha = 1, 2, \ldots, S \tag{5.18}$$

depends both on variables with label α and on all other variables, while

$$\frac{\partial u^\alpha}{\partial x_i^\alpha} > 0, \quad \alpha = 1, 2, \ldots, S, \quad i = 1, 2, \ldots, n,$$

$$\frac{\partial u^\alpha}{\partial x_i^\nu} \leq 0, \quad \alpha \neq \nu, \quad \alpha, \nu = 1, 2, \ldots, S, \quad i = 1, 2, \ldots, n.$$

Every consumer maximises his utility function, as was described in the previous Section, but now one ought to consider maximisation of S functions simultaneously. There is apparently no single point which gives maximum values for all functions simultaneously. However, one can exclude all points where values of utility functions can be enlarged simultaneously. The remaining points make up so-called Pareto-optimal set. No consumer in Pareto-optimal point can improve his/her welfare without diminishing someone's welfare. The problem of distribution of products among the members of the society was posed and investigated by Pareto (1909).

To find a Pareto-optimal set, one can construct a welfare function for whole community

$$U(x^1, x^2, \ldots, x^S) = \sum_{\nu=1}^{S} \alpha_\nu \, u^\nu(x^1, x^2, \ldots, x^S), \quad \alpha_\nu \geq 0, \quad \sum_{\nu=1}^{S} \alpha_\nu = 1.$$
(5.19)

A point of maximum of function 5.19 at arbitrary values of multipliers α_ν belong to the Pareto-optimal set.

One can use the Lagrange method for problem of maximisation of function 5.19 at restrictions 5.17 to find that Pareto-optimal points are obeyed to the set of equations

$$\sum_{\nu=1}^{S} \alpha_\nu \frac{\partial u^\nu}{\partial x_i^\mu} - p_i = 0, \quad \mu = 1, 2, \ldots, S; \quad i = 1, 2, \ldots, n,$$
(5.20)

where p_i is the Lagrange multipliers of the problem which are functions of the the multipliers α_ν.

One can reasonably assumes that the consumer's utility function depends only on his choice, so that relation 5.20 can be rewritten in a simpler form

$$\alpha_\nu \frac{\partial u^\nu}{\partial x_i^\nu} - p_i = 0, \quad \nu = 1, 2, \ldots, S; \quad i = 1, 2, \ldots, n.$$

So, for every consumer, one can write the relation

$$\frac{\partial u^\nu}{\partial x_i^\nu} : \frac{\partial u^\nu}{\partial x_j^\nu} = \frac{p_i}{p_j}, \quad \nu = 1, 2, \ldots, S; \quad i, j = 1, 2, \ldots, n$$
(5.21)

which coincides with relation 5.13. So the set of parameters coincides with a set of prices which are the same for all consumers.

Welfare function 5.19 is a function of amounts of products distributed among the members of the society. In line with this function, one can consider a function of the whole amounts of products

$$U(Q_1, Q_2, \ldots, Q_n), \quad Q_i = \sum_{\alpha=1}^{S} x_i^\alpha, \quad i = 1, 2, \ldots, n.$$

To relate this function to function 5.19, we assume that all consumers are in the same situation, that is, the quantity $x^\nu = Q/S$ does not depend on the index ν. Then,

$$\alpha_\nu \frac{\partial u^\nu}{\partial x^\nu_j} = \frac{\partial U}{\partial Q_j}, \quad \nu = 1, 2, \ldots, S; \quad j = 1, 2, \ldots, n.$$

One can see that the following relation is valid

$$\frac{\partial U}{\partial Q_i} : \frac{\partial U}{\partial Q_j} = \frac{p_i}{p_j}, \quad i, j = 1, 2, \ldots, n. \tag{5.22}$$

This is exactly relation 1.11 in which U is an objective utility function. So, one can consider the properties of welfare function as function of whole amounts of products to be similar to those of objective utility function introduced in Section 1.2. So, we can consider that, as characteristics of a set of products, the objective utility function and the welfare function are indistinguishable. Though objective utility function is not the value of a set of products, nevertheless, one can expect that the function is connected with the estimations of value.

5.5 Free-Price Market

Not only a separate individual, but a group of people, or even a society as a whole can be considered as an economic agent. Further on in Sections 5.4 and 5.5, we shall consider a very simple case, when each sector of production system is a producer and there is a single consumer, society in a whole. It allows us to find equations for the prices.

To consider a special example in more detail, we assume that the economy consists of n producers - each sector is a separate producer which output a single product - and the only consumer, the society as a whole. So, one ought to consider $n + 1$ economic agents, everyone of which has its own aims, plans its activity, and can take decisions.

The aim of the sector is to obtain a bigger amount of production of value Z^j. To imitate the behaviour of the sector, one ought to solve a maximisation problem, that is, to find amount of gross output which determines the greatest value of Z^j. We refer to the results of Section 3.3 to say that the gross output ought to be planned as big as possible at restriction given by basic fixed capital, so the supply functions for each product can be determined as functions of prices

$$Y_j^{\text{supply}}(\mathbf{p}) = Y_j(p_1, p_2, ..., p_n). \tag{5.23}$$

The aim of the society is to obtain the greatest usefulness from the products, that is, to find such quantities of output which would maximise a utility function. In this way, one can determine demand functions

$$Y_j^{\text{demand}}(\mathbf{p}, M) = Y_j(p_1, p_2, ..., p_n, M). \tag{5.24}$$

So, the problem of simultaneous maximisation of $n + 1$ objective functions is reduced to the problem of simultaneous consideration of the demand and supply functions for each product. One can consider each product separately and introduce an excess demand function

$$Z_j(\mathbf{p}, M) = Y_j^{\text{demand}}(\mathbf{p}, M) - Y_j^{\text{supply}}(\mathbf{p}), \tag{5.25}$$

where in contrast to what will be considered in the next Section, one assumes that there is only one price for each product on the market.

In situations which one calls *economic equilibrium*,[2] demand is equal to supply, so that

$$Z_j(\mathbf{p}, M) = 0, \quad j = 1, 2, \ldots, n. \tag{5.26}$$

This system of equations defines *equilibrium prices* whereas it is assumed that demand and supply functions have such dependencies of prices, that a stable solution of system 5.26 exists. One can consider the demand and supply functions of the chosen product as functions of the own price only. Situations in the market, as it has usually been considered, is depicted on the plot (Fig. 14), where one can see demand and supply curves.

---

[2]Economic equilibrium assumes that all macroeconomic variables which define economic system are constant, to say nothing of fluctuations. It reminds the definition of equilibrium in thermodynamics: all thermodynamic variables are constant on average, though there is movement of constituent particles of the thermodynamic system. Similarly, material constituent of economic system at equilibrium is not in thermodynamic equilibrium: there are processes of production and consumption of products. Economic equilibrium is an idealisation of reality which was stressed many times (Kornai, 1975), nevertheless it is a very useful idealisation, as well as thermodynamic equilibrium in physics.

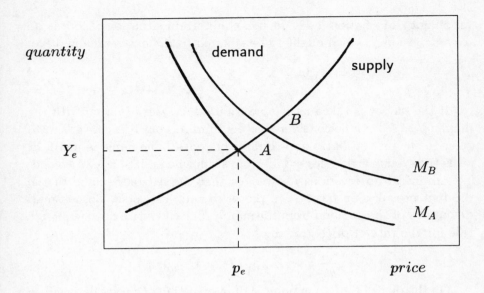

Figure 14 Situations on a free-price market of single product

The intersection of the demand and supply curves determines an equilibrium point (p_e, Y_e). At $M_B > M_A$, the demand increases and a new equilibrium price and a new equilibrium quantity which are greater than the previous ones appear.

The conditions for equilibrium prices can be written in the form of the Walras law

$$\sum_{i=1}^{n} p_i \, Z_i \, (\mathsf{p}, \, M) = 0. \tag{5.27}$$

The last relation defines equilibrium prices $p_j \geq 0$, if the relation is valid at $Z_i(\mathsf{p}) \leq 0$. The existence of system of prices is connected with behaviour of the excess demand functions $Z_i(\mathsf{p})$. So as we rely on the empirical observation that equilibrium prices exist, the problem is in defining of a class of functions which can describe demand and supply. The problem was studied in many details (Intriligator, 1971).

The essential component of real market is money which is considered as special commodity. An amount of money M ought to correspond to the value of the commodities in the sense which was discussed in Section 2.5. Relation 5.27 is valid for equilibrium situations and is an analogy of relation 2.28. In non-equilibrium situations there is an excess of money which ought to be equated to the excess demand

$$\Delta M = \sum_{i=1}^{n} p_i \, Z_i \, (\mathbf{p}, \, M). \tag{5.28}$$

If the money is taken as a separate product, the situation with the demand excess can be considered as equilibrium, but it is convenient to refer to such situation as non-equilibrium ones. The name is justified, so as the system strives for equilibrium state when relation 5.27 is valid.

Empirical observations assured us that the excess demand of the product provokes an increase in the price and vice versa. So, at small deviations of the demand from the supply, one can write down a simple rule for the rate of price growth

$$\frac{dp_i}{dt} = k_i \, Z_i \, (\mathbf{p}, \, M), \quad k_i \geq 0. \tag{5.29}$$

On the plot of Fig. 14, a point A of intersection of curves determines the equilibrium price and quantity. The excess or shortage of money causes a displacement of the demand curve up $(M_B > M_A)$ or down $(M_B < M_A)$. A new point B of equilibrium appears, whereas the price and quantity takes new values. However, the trajectory of the approach to the equilibrium point can differ from straight line and can resemble a cobweb, as it is described elsewhere (Allen, 1963).

Thus, the money excess provokes changes of prices, which can be determined with help of relations 5.28 and 5.29. One ought to know demand and supply functions to determine these changes. However, in the case when one restricts oneself by investigation of systems which includes the only sector which needs money, the situation is simple. One can assume, that in the case of discussed four-sector model, money is only needed for products of the fourth sector. So, equations 5.28 and 5.29 can be rewritten as

$$\frac{dM}{dt} = p_4 \, Z_4 \, (p_1, p_2, p_3, p_4, M),$$

$$\frac{dp_4}{dt} = k_4 \, Z_4 \, (p_1, p_2, p_3, p_4, M).$$

One can see that these equations are followed by a simple relation

$$\frac{dp_4^2}{dt} = 2 \, k_4 \, \frac{dM}{dt}. \tag{5.30}$$

The rate of growth of the squared price of consumer commodities is equal to the amount of emitted money.

5.6 Fixed-Price Market

In the cases, when there is a monopoly on the production of all commodities, a fixed price of the commodity can be set. It is a case of *centrally planned economy* designed in communist countries, where the state is the only owner of the whole production sector. Analysis shows (Voslenskii, 1984) that the real owner of the production is a *nomenclature class* which governed the economy on the behalf of the communist state.

As in the previous Section, we consider a market where n producing sectors and the only consumer are participating. We believe that the economic agents are characterised by demand and supply functions 5.23 and 5.24, but, in contrast to assumption in the previous Section, we suppose that the each product has, generally speaking, two prices: a wholesale price p' for the producer and a retail price p'' for the consumer. Existence of the two sets of prices is, according to Polterovich (1990, p. 185), 'a phenomenon of centrally planned economy'. So, instead of function 5.25, to describe a situation on the market, one ought to introduce an excess demand function which, in contrast to function in the previous section, depends on the two sets of prices.

$$Z_j\left(\mathbf{p}', \mathbf{p}'', M\right) = Y_j^{\text{demand}}(\mathbf{p}'', M) - Y_j^{\text{supply}}(\mathbf{p}'). \qquad (5.31)$$

Instead of 5.26, equilibrium situations are defined by relations

$$Z_j\left(\mathbf{p}', \mathbf{p}'', M\right) = 0, \quad j = 1, 2, \dots, n. \qquad (5.32)$$

The deeper sense of two-price-set market for the owner, the state, is to obtain income which is equal to

$$\sum_{i=1}^{n} \left(p_i'' - p_i'\right) Y_i. \qquad (5.33)$$

The communist state declares (and has the means to persuade its citizens) that the state's (or one can read: the nomenclature's) interests are the most important ones, so that in addition to the optimisation criteria for each participant of the market, considered in the previous section, the situation on the market is determined by the requirement of maximisation of quantity 5.33 as well.

Though the state controls the prices, the fixed prices p_i' and p_i'' cannot be set quite arbitrarily. One can see that system 5.32 can determine a set of equilibrium retail prices, if a set of the wholesale prices are given, and vice versa. Apart of it, the enterprises of production system keep some independence and interest to obtain profit. It is provoked by the requirements of finance self-supporting of each enterprise. So, the wholesale prices are fixed at such levels that enterprises (at least, some) have to obtain a moderate profit.

The equilibrium quantity of the product which is being sold and bought can be less or greater of co-ordinates of point of intersection of demand and supply curves (true equilibrium value which could be reached in the free-price market), as it is shown on plots of Fig. 15. It is well known fact (Polterovich, 1990) that there are commodities of both types in a centrally planned economy. Initial equilibrium situations for different products are depicted with lines $A'' - A'$ and $A' - A''$. In the one case, at $p'' > p'$, the state gets profit, which is called the turnover tax, in the other case, at $p' > p''$, the state is urged to subsidise the poor sectors.

It is supposed above, that in equilibrium situation there is no excess or deficit of money. In non-equilibrium case, instead of 5.32, one ought to write down relation

$$\Delta M = \sum_{i=1}^{n} p_i'' \, Z_i \left(\mathsf{p}', \mathsf{p}'', M \right). \tag{5.34}$$

The excess of money provokes crossover to a new equilibrium situation (line $B'' - B'$ in Fig. 15 (top) and $B' - B''$ in Fig. 15 (bottom)) which has to be determined by the state, so as it controls both production and prices. To begin with, the state usually announces some changes in wholesale prices. This announcement is accompanied by statements that the decision does not concern the retail prices. Despite the statements, after some time, the retail prices go up.[3]

---

[3] As a witness I can confirm the last assertions.

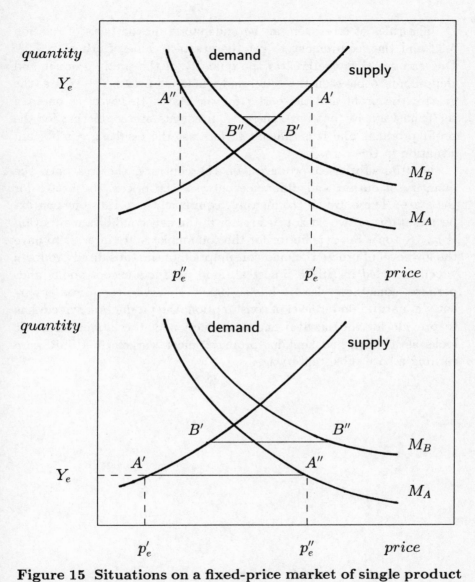

Figure 15 Situations on a fixed-price market of single product

Top: Subsided product. A wholesale price is greater than a retail price $(p'_e > p''_e)$ and the government urged to pay subside $(p'_e - p''_e) Y_e$ to the sector.
Bottom: Profit product. A wholesale price is less than a retail price $(p'_e < p''_e)$ and the government obtain profit $(p''_e - p'_e) Y_e$.

The rules of crossover can be understood on the basis of relation 5.32 and the requirement to get the greatest value of criterion 5.33. One can see that the greater the quantity of the profit product and the difference between the retail and wholesale prices $p'' - p'$ are, the greater the profit and the better for the state. However, as one can see from Fig. 15 (bottom), these requirements are conflicting for the profit products and it is difficult to forecast the resulting equilibrium situation in this case.

For the subsidised products, on the contrary, the less both the quantity of output and difference between the prices, the better for the state. These are not conflicting requirements, so that one can expect that output would not be greater in the new equilibrium situation (Fig. 15, top). So, it is better for the communist state interest to have the low level of production and consumption of the subsidised products which included in USSR almost all food products except vodka and, perhaps, something else (Rakitski, 1990). However, there was apparently a 'natural' lower level of consumption; the production system has to provide for the survival and reproduction of the labour force. It looks as if Marx had kept his promise: most workers in USSR were earning a bare subsistence wage.

6 Production of Value

In this Chapter we consider relationship between production of value and original (prime) sources of value, so called production factors. We have two alternative starting points. From one side, increase in production of value can be connected with increase in production equipment (capital), as it follows from input-output relations (Chapter 3), so that relation 6.2 can be written. From the other side, production of value, which can be associated with production of order in our close environment (see Section 1.2), is connected with increase in technological work, that is, increase in consumption of labour and energy, as it was discussed in Chapter 4. In all, we have three production factors to consider, while marginal productivities of capital, labour and energy are expressed through each other. Approximation of utility function allow us to find explicit forms of marginal productivities. The role of production factors different: labour and energy are the true sources of value. Capital is the means through which the labour resource is substituted by energy rather than a production factor itself. Capital and work are compliments to each other, while energy and labour inputs act as substitutes to each other.

6.1 Law of Substitution and Marginal Productivities

It was shown in Chapter 3 that increase in production of value is connected with increase in production equipment by simple formula 3.46, so increase in final output can be written as

$$dY = \sum_{i=1}^{n} \xi^i \, dK^i, \quad \xi^i = \sum_{j=1}^{n} \xi^i_j, \qquad (6.1)$$

where ξ^i_j are the capital marginal productivities relating to fundamental technological matrices A and B by formulae 3.46. As well as components of technological matrices, the marginal productivities depend on time. One can consider the production system to be a one-sector

107

system, so that for aggregate output (GDP) one has

$$dY = \xi \, dK, \tag{6.2}$$

where ξ is marginal productivity of capital, which is assumed to be positive quantity. As a consequence of 'stylised empirical facts of growth', the quantity is believed to be constant (Scott, 1989, p. 74), though, in fact, it is a subject to fluctuation. As an example, capital marginal productivity for US economy is shown in Fig. 16. It is a highly pulsating quantity, especially before year 1950. For years 1950 – 90, the mean values of the marginal productivity and its slope can be estimated as

$$\xi = 0.391 \; year^{-1}, \quad \frac{d\xi}{dt} = -0.00374 \; year^{-2}. \tag{6.3}$$

However, the production equipment is dead without labour and energy. It is known that the most important production factor appears to be labour, that is, a work of human being during the production of commodities. It was noted already in Chapter 4 that productivity of labour, that is, value of commodities produced by unit of labour in unit of time Y/L is increasing function of time. There is no doubt that developing of machine technologies appears to give an increase in labour productivity. However, to take into account the production equipment, we use the consumed in production energy E instead of variable K on the ground which was already discussed in Chapter 4.[1]

---

[1]To understand how consumed energy affects on the value of products, let us imagine development of an enterprise. One can consider that before a certain moment of time the technology which require some amount, L and E, of production factors were used, and then after changing the technology to produce the same quantity of the same product, the quantities $L - \Delta L$ and $E + \Delta E$ of production factor must be used. So as the products are considered to be identical, the exchange value of the product on the same market does not change, however, the amount of the whole value increased if the amount of labour L is used. So, one can see that value cannot be determined by labour only, a work by external sources ought; to be taken into account. The decrease of labourer's work is compensated by the work of external sources, so we can write the relation

$$-\beta \, \Delta L + \gamma \, \Delta E = 0,$$

where marginal productivities of production factors β and γ are introduced. It is easy to understand, that marginal productivities are determined not only by the technology, but also by market conditions.

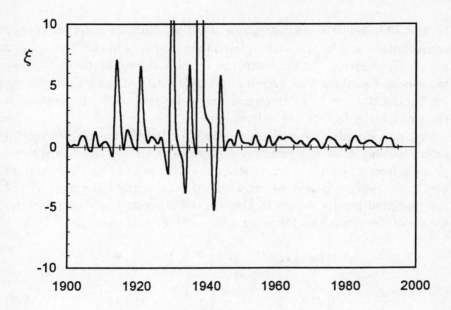

Figure 16 Marginal productivity of capital

The curve represent direct estimates for the US according to equation 6.2.

Although one needs production equipment (capital) to attract extra amount of external energy, work can be replaced only by work not by capital. The capital is an intermediate agent to attract energy. Productivity of capital is, in fact, productivity of energy. So we assume that the most natural variable has to be the amount of energy used in production E, not fixed capital.

Now we can discuss relationship between production factors and production of value. From one side, we have the work done by labour L and energy E, from the other side we have results: a set of products estimated to have exchange value Y. So, we can write down the relation between differentials of the quantities[2]

$$dY = \beta(L, E)\, dL + \gamma(L, E)\, dE. \qquad (6.4)$$

The written relation can be considered to be an expression of a substitution law. Quantities β and γ correspond to value produced

---

[2]Compare with equation 1.12.

by the addition of a unit of labour input at constant external energy consumption and by the addition of a unit of energy at constant labour input, respectively. In line with the existing economic theories these values can be labelled as marginal productivities of the corresponding production factors. The marginal productivities are both positive, if the production factors are independent.

As an example, one can use the data for the US (see Appendix) to calculate and draw marginal productivities β and γ which in dimensionless form are depicted as functions of time in Fig 17. The marginal productivities are pulsating functions of time, while the bigger one of the marginal productivities is, the less the other and vice versa. Mean values of the quantities for years 1950 – 90 are estimated as

$$\beta \frac{L}{K} = 0.848 \; year^{-1}, \quad \frac{d}{dt}\left(\beta \frac{L}{K}\right) = -0.035 \; year^{-2},$$

$$\gamma \frac{E}{K} = 0.219 \; year^{-1}, \quad \frac{d}{dt}\left(\gamma \frac{E}{K}\right) = 0.013 \; year^{-2}. \qquad (6.5)$$

Thus, one has two alternative expressions for production of value through production factors. We shall use formulae 6.2 and 6.4 as starting point of the theory of the productivity to obtain relations between marginal productivities of capital from the one side and of labour and energy from the other side (see formulae 6.22).

As well as capital consists of many parts with their own productivity, labour and energy can be divided into separate parts according to their quality, so that equation 6.4 can be generalised. In this Chapter, however, we shall use the simplest approach.

It was discovered by Marx (1867), that labour is such a commodity that gives surplus value. In our notations Marx's statement can be written as

$$(\beta - w)\,dL > 0,$$

where w is the price of labour (see Section 4.4). To explain the modern surplus in industrial societies, one ought to take the other production factor, energy, E into account and write down

$$(\beta - w)\,dL + (\gamma - p)\,dE > 0, \qquad (6.6)$$

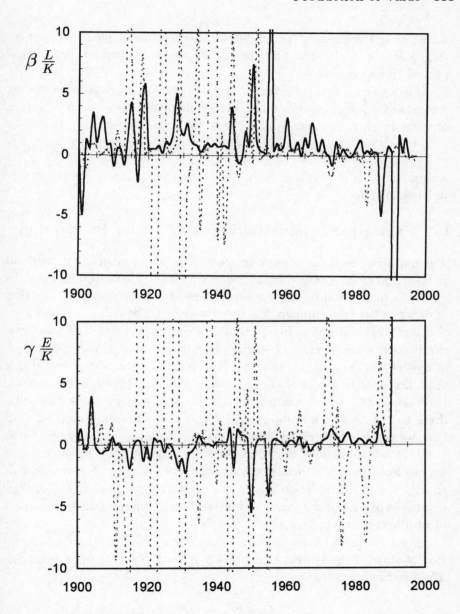

Figure 17 Marginal productivities of labour and energy

Solid curves represent direct estimates for the US economy according to equation 6.4. Dotted curves show results of calculation according to equation 6.22.

where p is the price of production consumption of energy (see Section 4.5). Both the first and the second terms in formula 6.6 are expected to be positive.

It is assumed in this Section that production of value is measured by a constant value unit. Otherwise, price index ρ appears, and production of value in current money units has to be written as

$$d\hat{Y} = \rho \, (dY)_\rho + \hat{Y} \, d\ln\rho, \tag{6.7}$$

where $(dY)_\rho$ is production of value at constant prices, given by above written formulae.

6.2   Marginal Productivities and U-order Production

The material result of production are buildings and machinery, cars and planes, and many other things among which the human being lives. In general words, production transformation of matter results in creation of order in the environment, the order which can be called U-order (see Section 1.2). So, one can say, that from a general point of view, the production system creates U-order in our environment, which has form of dissipative structures. To create and maintain the dissipative structure, fluxes of matter and energy must be coming through the system. In other words, to say nothing of the fluxes of matter, work has to be done to create and maintain order. One can see from equation 1.12 that total work determines production of utility or negoentropy of system. In our situation, the total work is work done by labourers and by mechanisms which use external sources of energy. So, the flux of energy is divided into two fluxes: biologically organised flux of energy (human work L) and socially organised flux of energy (work by means of production equipment E).

The U-order is characteristics of the system, so that there is a function of state of the system to characterise the U-order, utility function. The production of order

$$\dot{U} = \sum_{j=1}^{n} \frac{\partial U}{\partial Q_j} \dot{Q}_j$$

ought to be connected with production factors

$$\dot{U} = \dot{U}(L, E). \tag{6.8}$$

From the other side, the material result of production is characterised by value, so one can speak about production of value, which is connected by relation 6.4 with consumption of labour and energy. Relation 6.4 does not mean that in any case there is a certain $Y = Y(L, E)$ function. It is known (Korn and Korn, 1968) that condition

$$\frac{\partial \beta(L, E)}{\partial E} = \frac{\partial \gamma(L, E)}{\partial L}$$

must be fulfilled for linear form 6.4 to be the total differential of function $Y(L, E)$. However, in any case form 6.4 can be multiplied by a certain function which is called an integration factor, so that instead of the linear form 6.4 we have a total differential of a certain function which, according to formulae 6.8, can be identified with a function of production of order

$$d\dot{U} = \frac{\beta}{\psi} \, dL + \frac{\gamma}{\psi} \, dE. \tag{6.9}$$

We see that the integrating multiplier changes the production of value, which is not the function of system state, into the function $\dot{U}(L, E)$ which can be considered as a measure of a wholesome order produced during the unit of time.

To find an approximation of the utility function, we write down the differential 6.9 of function in the form

$$du = \beta^*(l, e) \, dl + \gamma^*(l, e) \, de,$$

where

$$u = \ln \frac{\dot{U}}{\dot{U}_0}, \quad l = \ln \frac{L}{L_0}, \quad e = \ln \frac{E}{E_0}.$$

Dimensionless marginal productivities β^* and γ^* can be expanded into series in power of small variables l and e

$$\beta^* = \beta_0 + \beta_l l + \beta_e e + \dots, \quad \gamma^* = \gamma_0 + \gamma_l l + \gamma_e e + \dots, \tag{6.10}$$

while, in virtue of condition of existence of utility function,

$$\beta_e = \gamma_l.$$

The zero-order terms of expansion 6.10 determine approximation of utility function in the form

$$\dot{U} = \dot{U}_0 \left(\frac{L}{L_0}\right)^{\beta_0} \left(\frac{E}{E_0}\right)^{\gamma_0}. \tag{6.11}$$

In this case the marginal productivities can be written as

$$\beta = \psi \frac{\dot{U}}{L} \beta_0, \qquad \gamma = \psi \frac{\dot{U}}{E} \gamma_0. \tag{6.12}$$

One can expect that the utility function for a large system must be a homogenous, uniform function of first order, that is

$$\dot{U}(\lambda L, \lambda E) = \lambda \dot{U}(L, E).$$

Under this condition instead of function 6.11 we write down

$$\dot{U} = \dot{U}_0 \frac{L}{L_0} \Xi^\alpha, \tag{6.13}$$

where $\alpha = \gamma_0 = 1 - \beta_0$, and we have introduced the following quantity

$$\Xi = \frac{L_0}{L} \frac{E}{E_0}. \tag{6.14}$$

In this situation the integrating multiplier can also be represented by a power function

$$\psi \sim \Xi^q,$$

so that from relations 6.12 – 6.13, one obtains an approximation of marginal productivities[3]

---

[3]A better approximation can be obtained, if one uses the first-order terms of expansion 6.10 to determine first-order function

$$\dot{U} = \dot{U}_0 \left(\frac{L}{L_0}\right)^{\beta_0} \left(\frac{E}{E_0}\right)^{\gamma_0} \exp \frac{1}{2} \left(\beta_l \ln^2 \frac{L}{L_0} + (\beta_e + \gamma_l) \ln \frac{L}{L_0} \ln \frac{E}{E_0} + \gamma_e \ln^2 \frac{E}{E_0}\right)$$

which under condition of uniformity is written as

$$\dot{U} = \dot{U}_0 \frac{L}{L_0} \Xi^\alpha \exp \left(\frac{1}{2} b \ln^2 \Xi\right), \quad b = -\beta_l = \beta_e = \gamma_l = -\gamma_e.$$

$$\beta = Q \frac{1 - \alpha}{L_0} \Xi^{q+\alpha}, \qquad \gamma = Q \frac{\alpha}{E_0} \Xi^{q+\alpha-1}. \tag{6.15}$$

The constant Q is determined by initial conditions; however, the quantities q and α are quite arbitrary ones, if there is no requirement on properties of the marginal productivities. If one consider the marginal productivities to be increasing functions of the ratio energy/labour, while increase of marginal productivity of energy decreases when the ratio increases, that is

$$\frac{d\beta}{d\Xi} > 0, \quad \frac{d\gamma}{d\Xi} > 0, \quad \frac{d^2\gamma}{d\Xi^2} < 0,$$

one gets some restrictions for parameters

$$0 < \alpha < 1 < q + \alpha < 2.$$

Taking relations 6.15 into account, equation 6.4 can be rewritten in the form

$$dY = Q \frac{1 - \alpha}{L_0} \left(\frac{L_0}{L} \frac{E}{E_0} \right)^{q+\alpha} dL + Q \frac{\alpha}{E_0} \left(\frac{L_0}{L} \frac{E}{E_0} \right)^{q+\alpha-1} dE. \tag{6.16}$$

One can see that only in the case if $q = 0$, there exists a production function $Y(L, E)$ which in the first approximation has the form

$$Y = Y_0 \frac{L}{L_0} \left(\frac{L_0}{L} \frac{E}{E_0} \right)^{\alpha}. \tag{6.17}$$

This function has the exact form of the neo-classical, namely, Cobb-Douglas production function in which capital K stands for energy E.

In general case, production of value Y is not any function of the variables L and E at the same time, as it can be proposed. The production of value can be represented as a function of the variables at the previous moments of time, i.e. a function of a trajectory of evolution

$$Y(t) = Y_{s=-\infty}^t [L(s), E(s)]. \tag{6.18}$$

For every known dependence of $L(t)$ and $E(t)$, the production of value $Y(t)$ can be found from formula 6.16.

6.3   Marginal Productivities and Technological Coefficients

Now we again refer to expressions 6.2 and 6.4 for production of value which can be rewritten in the form

$$\frac{dY}{dt} = \xi \, \frac{dK}{dt}, \qquad \frac{dY}{dt} = \beta \, \frac{dL}{dt} + \gamma \, \frac{dE}{dt}, \qquad (6.19)$$

while the rates of growth of the production factors are defined by equations 4.15, that is,

$$\frac{dK}{dt} = I - \mu K, \qquad \frac{dL}{dt} = \lambda \, I - \mu L, \qquad \frac{dE}{dt} = \varepsilon \, I - \mu E. \qquad (6.20)$$

The technological coefficients λ and ε characterise a level of applied technology. It was shown in Chapter 4 that the dimensionless technological variables

$$\bar{\lambda} = \lambda K / L, \qquad \bar{\varepsilon} = \varepsilon K / E$$

are determined by equations 4.40 and 4.41. These quantities are endogenous characteristics which are considered to be functions of time.

We combine equations 6.19 and 6.20 to rewrite production of value in the form

$$\frac{dY}{dt} = \xi \, (I - \mu \, K), \qquad \frac{dY}{dt} = (\beta \, \lambda + \gamma \, \varepsilon) \, I - \mu \, (\beta \, L + \gamma \, E). \qquad (6.21)$$

We can compare these equations to find the relation between characteristic parameters of the system

$$\beta \, \lambda + \gamma \, \varepsilon \;=\; \xi,$$

$$\beta \, L + \gamma \, E \;=\; \xi \, K.$$

The latter relations can be considered to be a set of equations for the marginal productivities β and ε. So, one can find

$$\xi = \beta \, \frac{L}{K} + \gamma \, \frac{E}{K}, \qquad \beta = \xi \, \frac{\bar{\varepsilon} - 1}{\bar{\varepsilon} - \bar{\lambda}} \, \frac{K}{L}, \qquad \gamma = \xi \, \frac{1 - \bar{\lambda}}{\bar{\varepsilon} - \bar{\lambda}} \, \frac{K}{E}. \qquad (6.22)$$

One can see that marginal productivities are positive, if

$$\bar{\lambda} < 1 < \bar{\varepsilon} \quad or \quad \bar{\lambda} > 1 > \bar{\varepsilon}. \tag{6.23}$$

However, it is possible that one of the marginal productivities is negative. But they cannot be both negative.

After having equated expressions 6.15 and 6.22 for marginal productivities, one obtains

$$\xi = Q\frac{L}{L_0 K}\Xi^{q+\alpha}, \qquad \alpha = \frac{1 - \bar{\lambda}}{\bar{\varepsilon} - \bar{\lambda}}. \tag{6.24}$$

In virtue of these formulae, the relation 4.20 between different rates of growth can be written as

$$\delta = \nu + \alpha\,(\eta - \nu). \tag{6.25}$$

Now relation 6.2 can be rewritten in the form

$$dY = Q\frac{L}{L_0 K}\left(\frac{L_0}{L}\frac{E}{E_0}\right)^{q+\alpha} dK, \qquad \alpha = \frac{1 - \bar{\lambda}}{\bar{\varepsilon} - \bar{\lambda}}. \tag{6.26}$$

The constant Q is determined by initial conditions, so that the only parameter which remains unknown in the expressions for marginal productivities, to say nothing of the initial values of variables, is the quantity q. To find a formula for estimation of this quantity, we start with differentiating the first equation of 6.24 at $\alpha = const$, $q = const$ and after some simple operations, one determines the unknown quantity as

$$q = \frac{1}{\bar{\varepsilon} - \bar{\lambda}}\frac{K}{I}\frac{1}{\xi}\frac{d\xi}{dt}. \tag{6.27}$$

In a simple case, when potential rates of growth of the production factors are constant, that is $\tilde{\delta} = \delta$, $\tilde{\nu} = \nu$, $\tilde{\eta} = \eta$, one has

$$\bar{\lambda} = \frac{\nu + \mu}{\delta + \mu}, \quad \bar{\varepsilon} = \frac{\eta + \mu}{\delta + \mu}, \quad \alpha = \frac{\delta - \nu}{\eta - \nu}, \quad q = \frac{1}{\eta - \nu}\frac{1}{\xi}\frac{d\xi}{dt}$$

and the marginal productivities 6.22 take the form

$$\beta = \xi\frac{\eta - \delta}{\eta - \nu}\frac{K}{L}, \qquad \gamma = \xi\frac{\delta - \nu}{\eta - \nu}\frac{K}{E}.$$

In terms of the growth rates, the conditions of positivity are read

$$\nu < \delta < \eta \quad or \quad \nu > \delta > \eta. \tag{6.28}$$

One can see that relation 6.25 between the rates of growth of the production factors is an identity if rates of growth are constant. However, it is an important relation in the general case.

Formulae 6.22 allows us to calculate the marginal productivities β and γ if the quantities in the right hand side of formulae 6.22 are known. The dotted curves in Fig. 17 show estimates due to formulae 6.22 as compared with direct empirical estimates of marginal productivities. One can observe the coincidence of pulsations for some years and some discrepancies. However, one ought to refer to primary statistical data to discuss the reasons of discrepancies.

The empirical estimates of mean values can be compared with mean values of quantities calculated according to formulae 6.22

$$\beta \frac{L}{K} = 0.178 \, year^{-1}, \quad \gamma \frac{E}{K} = 0.419 \, year^{-1}. \tag{6.29}$$

One can be satisfied with coincidence of quantities within one decade, taking into account scattering of empirical data. One can see that the marginal productivities are positive both, though, for considered period 1950 – 90 years, according to previous estimations (see formulae 4.21), mean rates of growth $\nu < \eta < \delta$. However, the conditions of positivity are valid for strictly constant rates of growth. More comparisons are needed to be assured that the theory works properly.

One can use formulae 6.24, 6.27 and the previous estimates of different quantities (see formulae 4.17 and 6.3, whereas $I/K = 0.0923$), to obtain parameters for the US national economy in years 1950 – 90

$$\alpha = 1.045, \quad q = -0.457. \tag{6.30}$$

6.4   The Best Utilisation of Production Factors

One can assume that production factors are chosen in such amounts, so as they must be the most effective in production, that is, values of production factors maximise utility function at given total expenses for production factors. It means that one is interested in the maximum value of function $\dot{U}(L, E)$ at condition

$$wL + pE = V,$$

where w and p are prices of 'consumption' of production factors, and V is a part of gross output which goes for maintaince of production factors. It is clear that amount of value which is needed to suport energy E is equal to μK, so that price of consumption of energy is

$$p = \frac{\mu K}{E} \tag{6.31}$$

One can follow a general method of finding the conditional extremum (Korn and Korn, 1968), so that we look for the unconditional maximum of the Lagrange function

$$\dot{U}(L, E) - \kappa(wL + pE - V),$$

where κ is Lagrange multiplier.

So, we obtain equations for a point of the conditional extremum

$$\frac{\partial \dot{U}}{\partial L} = \kappa w, \quad \frac{\partial \dot{U}}{\partial E} = \kappa p.$$

One can use formula 6.9, to determine the marginal productivities

$$\beta = \psi(L, E)\kappa w, \quad \gamma = \psi(L, E)\kappa p.$$

From the last relations it follows, that ratio of prices of production factors is equal to the the ratio of marginal productivities or, referring to equations 6.22, is inversely proportional to the ratio of production factors

$$\frac{w}{p} = \frac{\beta}{\gamma} = \frac{\bar{\varepsilon} - 1}{1 - \bar{\lambda}} \frac{E}{L}. \tag{6.32}$$

We have obtained a relation between prices of production factors. Taking into account equation 6.31, one can define price of labour as

$$w = \mu \frac{\bar{\varepsilon} - 1}{1 - \bar{\lambda}} \frac{K}{L}. \tag{6.33}$$

It is not real wage which can include expanding accumulation, but part of it which is needed to compensate current cunsumption of humans.

One can see from equation 6.32 that the index $\alpha = \dfrac{1 - \bar{\lambda}}{\bar{\varepsilon} - \bar{\lambda}}$ can be expressed through prices and amounts of production factors

$$\alpha = \frac{pE}{wL + pE}. \tag{6.34}$$

So, the meaning of index α in the equilibrium situation can be defined as follows: it is a part of total expenses for production factors needed for utilisation of energy as a production factor. If production factors are chosen as optimal, then

$$0 < \alpha < 1 \tag{6.35}$$

which implies restrictions on values of technological variables

$$\bar{\lambda} < 1 < \bar{\varepsilon} \quad or \quad \bar{\lambda} > 1 > \bar{\varepsilon}.$$

These conditions coincide with conditions of positivity of marginal productivities (see formulae 6.23 and 6.28 in the previous Section).

One can see that, while marginal productivities for US economy are positive (see 6.5 and 6.29), quantity α is slightly more than unity (see 6.30). This discrepancy can be attributed to statistical scattering of data. Under these circumstances, different estimates give different results.

6.5   Index of Labour Productivity Growth

The obtained system of equations of economic growth allow us to introduce a global characteristic of labour efficiency. To find output $Y(t)$ at the given time t, we refer to expression 6.21 for production of value, which can be rewritten as

$$\frac{dY}{dt} = (\beta\lambda + \gamma\varepsilon)(I - \check{I}), \tag{6.36}$$

where

$$\check{I} = \mu \frac{\beta L + \gamma E}{\beta \lambda + \gamma \varepsilon} = \mu \frac{\beta L + \gamma E}{\beta \bar{\lambda} L + \gamma \bar{\varepsilon} E} K. \tag{6.37}$$

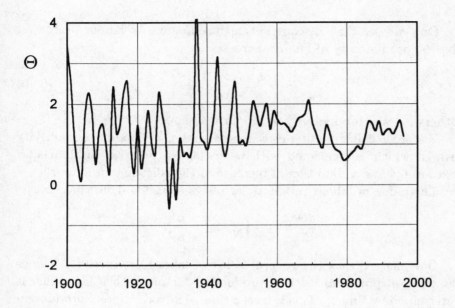

Figure 18 Index of labour productivity growth for the US

In the case when this quantity is greater than unity, the substitution of human work by the work of out-of-the-body natural sources occurs: the productivity of labour increases.

Both technological coefficients λ, ε and dimensionless technological variables

$$\bar{\lambda} = \lambda K/L, \qquad \bar{\varepsilon} = \varepsilon K/E$$

are functions of time.

At constant output, that is at $dY/dt = 0$, according to equations 6.36 and 6.37, investments are determined as

$$I = \mu \, \frac{\beta L + \gamma E}{\beta \lambda + \gamma \varepsilon}. \tag{6.38}$$

To obtain the condition of the labour productivity growth, according to relation 6.20, we write down the rates of growth of production factors

$$\frac{dL}{dt} = -\mu\gamma\frac{\varepsilon L - \lambda E}{\beta \lambda + \gamma \varepsilon}, \qquad \frac{dE}{dt} = \mu\beta\frac{\varepsilon L - \lambda E}{\beta \lambda + \gamma \varepsilon}. \tag{6.39}$$

One can see that, at constant output, amount of labour decreases, that is, productivity of labour increases if

$$\Theta = \frac{\bar{\varepsilon}}{\bar{\lambda}} = \frac{\varepsilon L}{\lambda E} > 1. \tag{6.40}$$

Otherwise, the productivity of labour decreases.

We shall call quantity Θ a general index of labour productivity growth which is connected with technological progress and consider relation 6.40 as a condition of increase of the efficiency of labour.

The index of labour productivity obeys equation 4.39, that is

$$\frac{d\Theta}{dt} = -\frac{1}{\tau}\left(\Theta - \frac{\tilde{\eta} + \mu}{\tilde{\nu} + \mu}\right). \tag{6.41}$$

One can see that the general index of labour productivity follows the ratio of potential rates of production factors with a lag which is determined by time τ. This time is a time of introduction of production equipment.

Formulae 4.19 allows one to write the index of technical progress in the form

$$\Theta = \frac{\eta + \mu}{\nu + \mu}. \tag{6.42}$$

It follows from this relation that, when 6.40 is valid,

$$\eta > \nu$$

which means that the rate of growth of consumption of energy exceed the rate of growth of labour, when technological progress has occurred.

Empirical values of quantity Θ are depicted in Fig. 18 for the United States economy. One can see that the index of technical progress is often considerably lower than 1, that indicates substitution of energy by labour in times of high or rising energy prices. However, the mean value of quantity is 1.35 or, if calculated as ratio of mean technological coefficients, 1.31, which testifies about labour productivity growth. The index seems to be strongly influenced by substitution processes due to changes in technology and in the factor prices. It appears to be a very sensitive index of the current technological situation.

7 One-Sector Approach to Economic Growth

In this Chapter we are collecting results of the previous Chapters to formulate a closed set of equations of economic growth. The development of the production system is eventually determined by growth of labour supply and by possibilities of attracting of extra amount of external energy, so that the set of evolution equations of production system contains two important quantities: potential rates of labour and energy growth, namely, $\tilde{\nu}(t)$ and $\tilde{\eta}(t)$, which, in principle, are endogenous characteristics in problem of evolution of human population (see Sections 4.4 and 4.5). We shall consider these quantities to be given as exogenous characteristics in the system of equations of economic growth. This is a system of evolution equations, so that initial values of all variables have to be given. Apart from it, three internal parameters: index of capital productivity growth q, rate of depreciation μ and time of technological rearrangement τ as inherent characteristics of the production system have to be given. The formulated equations allow one to calculate and draw trajectories of development of the economic system for given values of available production factors. In the simplest case, when potential rates of production factors are constant, it is an exponential trajectory, which is shown to be a stable one. One can draw a picture of future development of the economy. However, we lay stress on the parameters that ought to be known in order to make a successful forecast, rather than on the forecast itself.

7.1 Equations of Economic Growth

Equation 6.21 gives us two equivalent forms of expressions for production of value

$$\frac{dY}{dt} = \xi \, (I - \mu \, K) = (\beta \, \lambda + \gamma \, \varepsilon) \, I - \mu \, (\beta \, L + \gamma \, E), \qquad (7.1)$$

where the marginal productivities ξ, β, and γ are connected with each other and defined in Sections 6.2 and 6.3 as

$$\xi = Q\frac{L}{L_0 K}\left(\frac{EL_0}{E_0 L}\right)^{q+\alpha}, \quad \beta = Q\frac{1-\alpha}{L_0}\left(\frac{EL_0}{E_0 L}\right)^{q+\alpha},$$

$$\gamma = Q\frac{\alpha}{E_0}\left(\frac{EL_0}{E_0 L}\right)^{q+\alpha-1}, \quad \alpha = \frac{1-\bar\lambda}{\bar\varepsilon-\bar\lambda}. \tag{7.2}$$

The constant Q is determined by initial conditions, the quantity q ought to be given as a measure of change of the marginal productivity of capital (see formula 6.27).

The rates of growth of the production factors are defined by equations 4.15, that is

$$\frac{dK}{dt} = I - \mu K, \quad \frac{dL}{dt} = \lambda\,I - \mu L, \quad \frac{dE}{dt} = \varepsilon\,I - \mu E. \tag{7.3}$$

The technological coefficient λ and ε characterise a level of applied technology. It was shown in Section 4.5 that the dimensionless technological variables

$$\bar\lambda = \lambda K/L, \qquad \bar\varepsilon = \varepsilon K/E$$

are determined by equations 4.40 and 4.41, that is

$$\frac{d\bar\lambda}{dt} = -\frac{1}{\tau}\left(\bar\lambda - \frac{\tilde\nu+\mu}{\tilde\delta+\mu}\right), \quad \frac{d\bar\varepsilon}{dt} = -\frac{1}{\tau}\left(\bar\varepsilon - \frac{\tilde\eta+\mu}{\tilde\delta+\mu}\right), \tag{7.4}$$

where τ is time of crossover from one technological situation to another. It is determined by internal processes of developing of technology. In addition to parameter τ, the rate of depreciation μ and index of capital productivity growth q have to be given as well.

These relation ought to be completed by definition of investments 4.37, that is

$$\frac{I}{K} = \chi + \min\begin{cases} (\tilde\delta+\mu) \\ (\tilde\nu+\mu)/\bar\lambda \ , \\ (\tilde\eta+\mu)/\bar\varepsilon \end{cases} \tag{7.5}$$

where χ is a share of governmental investment.

The potential rate of capital growth $\tilde\delta(t)$ appears to be an variable which is determined by equation 4.58, that is,

$$\frac{d\tilde\delta}{dt} = -\frac{1}{\tau}\left(\tilde\delta - \tilde\nu - \alpha\left(\tilde\eta - \tilde\nu\right)\right). \tag{7.6}$$

If one assumes that potential rates of labour and energy growth $\tilde{\nu}(t)$ and $\tilde{\eta}(t)$ are given as exogenous functions of time, the above equations represent a closed set of equations for the variables Y, L, E, K, I, $\bar{\lambda}$, $\bar{\varepsilon}$, and $\tilde{\delta}$, while internal parameters q, μ and τ have to be given. Equations 7.1 – 7.6 describe the evolution of the economic system, so that initial values of all variables have to be given.

The potential rates of growth of labour and energy ought to be considered as endogenous quantities in the problem of evolution of the human population (see Sections 4.4 and 4.5) and can be determined by formulae 4.27 and 4.34. The potential rate of labour supply growth $\tilde{\nu}$ can be related to rate of population growth. In the simplest case, we can consider functions $f(w)$ in relation 4.22 to be constant and to be equal to 0.5, so that according to formula 4.27, the potential rate of labour growth is

$$\tilde{\nu} = b - d. \tag{7.7}$$

However, we have failed to connect the potential rate of energy growth with other variables: we know nothing about function 4.31 and we cannot calculate the potential rate of energy growth through stock of knowledge, so that in any case quantity $\tilde{\eta}(t)$ ought to be given as a function of time.

7.2 Exponential Growth

Assuming that rates of potential growth of production factors are given, the set of equations 7.1 – 7.6 can be applied to complicated cases. However, as an example, and to test the theory, we shall apply it to the simple case, when the potential rates of growth of production factors are given as constant, that is

$$\tilde{\delta} = \delta, \quad \tilde{\nu} = \nu, \quad \tilde{\eta} = \eta.$$

We can see that in this case equations 7.4 and 7.5 are followed by asymptotic relations between investments and the technological coefficients from one side and rates of growth from the other side

$$I = (\delta + \mu)K, \qquad \lambda = \frac{\nu + \mu}{\delta + \mu}\frac{L}{K}, \qquad \varepsilon = \frac{\eta + \mu}{\delta + \mu}\frac{E}{K}. \tag{7.8}$$

Then, it is easy to see that equations 7.3 have a solution in the form of exponential functions of time

$$K = K_0 e^{\delta t}, \qquad L = L_0 e^{\nu t}, \qquad E = E_0 e^{\eta t}. \qquad (7.9)$$

Now, we use relations 7.1 and 7.9, to obtain the following expression for output[1]

$$Y = Y_0 e^{[\nu + (q+\alpha)(\eta-\nu)]t} = Y_0 e^{[\delta + q(\eta-\nu)]t}, \qquad (7.10)$$

where

$$Y_0 = \frac{\nu + \alpha(\eta - \nu)}{\nu + (q + \alpha)(\eta - \nu)} Q. \qquad (7.11)$$

We can apply this result to development of the US economy in years $1950 - 90$, when growth of production factors can be considered to be approximately exponential with rates of growth

$$\delta = 0.0427, \quad \nu = 0.0186, \quad \eta = 0.0371, \quad \mu = 0.05. \qquad (7.12)$$

Making use of the previously calculated values of q (formula 6.30), it is possible to find out the average rate of increase of the output for the reviewed period, i.e. 0.0342 instead of the empirical value 0.0309 shown in formula 2.7. The results of this comparison can be regarded as quite satisfactory, given the rough estimate of the parameters of the problem. Deviation of the rate of output growth from the rate of capital growth is connected with change of capital productivity. The resulting

---

[1]For comparison I should like to remind the reader, that if one uses neo-classical production function 1.23 in the Cobb-Douglas form

$$Y = Y_0 \frac{L}{L_0} \left(\frac{L_0}{L} \frac{K}{K_0} \right)^\alpha, \quad 0 < \alpha < 1$$

one could obtain output for trajectories 7.9

$$Y = Y_0 e^{[(1-\alpha)\nu + \alpha\delta]t}.$$

When one applies this result to explain empirical relations between rates of growth of different quantities, some contradictions, which were analysed by Solow (1957), appear (Blanchard and Fisher, 1989, p. 4). It is well known fact which has came to numerous modifications of production function 1.23 (Ferguson, 1969). However, Hannon and Joyce (1981) have shown that Cobb-Douglas production function describes data for the USA at $\alpha \approx 1$.

expression implies that the rate of increase of labour productivity is determined by the difference in the energy increase rate and the labour growth rate

$$(q + \alpha)(\eta - \nu) = \delta - \nu + q(\eta - \nu).$$

One can see that the theory describes the 'stylised' facts of economic growth, that is, exponential growth of output and production factors, whereas rates of growth are connected with each other.

Though there is a relation 4.20 between rates of growth of different production factors, that is

$$\delta = \nu + \alpha(\eta - \nu),$$

it is an identity in the case of constant rates of growth. So, all potential rates of growth can be set independently. Note that rate of capital growth δ can be considered to be eventually determined by the level of consumption

$$w = \frac{Y - I}{L} = \left(e^{q(\eta-\nu)t} - (\mu + \delta) \frac{K_0}{Y_0} \right) \frac{Y_0}{L_0} e^{(\delta-\nu)t}. \qquad (7.13)$$

One can see that a constant negative value of the quantity q would bring the consumption level to zero, which is intolerable. A situation, where the quantity q has a constant positive value is intolerable as well, as it would eventually bring investment down to zero. So, the quantity q is either constant and equal to zero or pulsating about zero.

The above relationship reveals that an increase in the rate of capital growth leads to an increase in the consumption level rate and to a decrease of current consumption. The relationship can be regarded as a basis for the choice of the worthwhile technological policy in 'pure exponents'. The higher the rate of capital growth, the more it pays to depress the current level of consumption in order to enjoy higher consumption later.

7.3 Stability of Exponential Trajectory

Now, we again refer to the system of equations of economic growth 7.1 – 7.6 which can be rewritten in a more compact form by introducing new variables, namely, labour productivity, energy availability, and investment ratio, respectively

$$y = \frac{Y}{L}, \quad \epsilon = \frac{E}{L}, \quad i = \frac{I}{K}.$$

Then, the equations of economic growth 7.1 – 7.6 take the form

$$\frac{dy}{dt} = (\beta(\epsilon) - y)(\bar{\lambda}\, i - \mu) + \gamma(\epsilon)(\bar{\varepsilon}\, i - \mu)\, \epsilon, \qquad \frac{d\epsilon}{dt} = i\,(\bar{\varepsilon} - \bar{\lambda})\, \epsilon,$$

$$i = \min\left\{ (\tilde{\delta} + \mu), \; (\tilde{\nu} + \mu)/\bar{\lambda}, \; (\tilde{\eta} + \mu)/\bar{\varepsilon} \right\},$$

$$\frac{d\bar{\lambda}}{dt} = -\frac{1}{\tau}\left(\bar{\lambda} - \frac{\tilde{\nu} + \mu}{\tilde{\delta} + \mu} \right), \qquad \frac{d\bar{\varepsilon}}{dt} = -\frac{1}{\tau}\left(\bar{\varepsilon} - \frac{\tilde{\eta} + \mu}{\tilde{\delta} + \mu} \right),$$

$$\frac{d\tilde{\delta}}{dt} = -\frac{1}{\tau}\left(\tilde{\delta} - \tilde{\nu} - \alpha\,(\tilde{\eta} - \tilde{\nu}) \right), \qquad \alpha = \frac{1 - \bar{\lambda}}{\bar{\varepsilon} - \bar{\lambda}}. \qquad (7.14)$$

The marginal productivitiies $\beta(\epsilon)$ and $\gamma(\epsilon)$ are characteristics of the system and ought to be given. In the simplest approximation according to relation 6.15

$$\beta(\epsilon) = k\, y_0\, (1 - \alpha) \left(\frac{\epsilon}{\epsilon_0} \right)^{q+\alpha}, \qquad \gamma(\epsilon) = k\, \frac{y_0}{\epsilon_0}\, \alpha \left(\frac{\epsilon}{\epsilon_0} \right)^{q+\alpha-1}, \qquad (7.15)$$

where $k = Q/Y_0$ is determined from initial conditions. For exponential trajectories, the ratio is given by formula 7.11.

Further on, we consider a case, when the potential rates of production factors can be represented as a sum of constant mean values and small time-dependent additions

$$\tilde{\delta} = \delta + \Delta\delta, \quad \tilde{\nu} = \nu + \Delta\nu, \quad \tilde{\eta} = \eta + \Delta\eta.$$

One can expect that in this case the trajectory of evolution would be close to the exponential one, investigated in Section 7.1. We shall consider deviations of the trajectory from solution 7.8 – 7.10 which can be rewritten in the form

$$y = y_0 e^{[\delta - \nu + q(\eta - \nu)]t}, \qquad \epsilon = \epsilon_0 e^{(\eta - \nu)t},$$

$$i = (\delta + \mu), \quad \bar{\lambda} = \frac{\nu + \mu}{\delta + \mu}, \quad \bar{\varepsilon} = \frac{\eta + \mu}{\delta + \mu}. \qquad (7.16)$$

One can assume that investments and the technological coefficients can be taken in the form

$$y = y_0(1+v)e^{[\delta - v + q(\eta - v)]t}, \quad \epsilon = \epsilon_0(1+u)e^{(\eta - v)t},$$

$$i = (\delta + \mu)(1 + G), \quad \bar{\lambda} = \frac{v + \mu}{\delta + \mu}(1 + B), \quad \bar{\varepsilon} = \frac{\eta + \mu}{\delta + \mu}(1 + H),$$

$$\alpha = \frac{\delta - v}{\eta - v} + \frac{(\mu + v)(\delta - \eta)}{(\eta - v)^2} B - \frac{(\mu + \eta)(\delta - v)}{(\eta - v)^2} H. \tag{7.17}$$

One can consider the quantities G, B, and H to be small ones, they are connected with the small increments of the rates of production factors according to equations

$$G = \min\left\{\frac{\Delta\delta}{\delta + \mu}, \frac{\Delta v}{v + \mu} - B, \frac{\Delta\eta}{\eta + \mu} - H\right\},$$

$$\frac{d\Delta\delta}{dt} = -\frac{1}{\tau}\left(\Delta\delta - \frac{(\mu + v)(\delta - \eta)}{(\eta - v)^2} B\right.$$

$$\left. + \frac{(\mu + \eta)(\delta - v)}{(\eta - v)^2} H + \frac{\delta - \eta}{\eta - v}\Delta v - \frac{\delta - v}{\eta - v}\Delta\eta\right),$$

$$\frac{dB}{dt} = -\frac{1}{\tau}\left(B - \frac{\Delta v}{v + \mu} + \frac{\Delta\delta}{\delta + \mu}\right),$$

$$\frac{dH}{dt} = -\frac{1}{\tau}\left(H - \frac{\Delta\eta}{\eta + \mu} + \frac{\Delta\delta}{\delta + \mu}\right). \tag{7.18}$$

According to equations 7.15 and 7.17 in the first approximation with respect to small quantities, one has the following expression for the marginal productivities

$$\beta(\epsilon) = k\, y_0\, (1 - \alpha)\, [1 + (\alpha + q)u]\, e^{(q+\alpha)(\eta - v)t},$$

$$\gamma(\epsilon) = k\, \frac{y_0}{\epsilon_0}\, \alpha\, [1 + (\alpha + q - 1)u]\, e^{(q+\alpha-1)(\eta - v)t}. \tag{7.19}$$

Here we consider α to have its non-perturbed value.

Now, on the basis of equations 7.14, one can write down a system of uniform equations for small increments in linear approximation

$$\frac{dv}{dt} = -[\delta + q(\eta - \nu)]\, v + (\alpha + q)\, [\delta + q(\eta - \nu)]\, u$$
$$+[(1 - \alpha)k - 1]\, \nu(\nu + \mu)\, (B + G) + \alpha k(\eta + \mu)\, (H + G),$$

$$\frac{du}{dt} = (\eta + \mu)\, (H + G) - (\nu + \mu)\, (B + G),$$

$$\frac{d\Delta\delta}{dt} = -\frac{1}{\tau} \left(\Delta\delta - \frac{(\mu + \nu)(\delta - \eta)}{(\eta - \nu)^2}\, B + \frac{(\mu + \eta)(\delta - \nu)}{(\eta - \nu)^2}\, H \right),$$

$$\frac{dB}{dt} = -\frac{1}{\tau}\, B,$$

$$\frac{dH}{dt} = -\frac{1}{\tau}\, H, \qquad G = \min\{0,\, -B,\, -H\}. \tag{7.20}$$

To consider stability, we use estimates 7.12 of the parameters for the US economy, so that we can rewrite the system of equations in the form

$$\frac{dv}{dt} = -0.0307\, v + 0.0378\, u - 0.001\, (B + G) + 0.0295\, (H + G),$$

$$\frac{du}{dt} = 0.1276\, (H + G) - 0.1143\, (B + G),$$

$$\frac{d\Delta\delta}{dt} = -\frac{1}{\tau} (\Delta\delta - 1.122\, B + 6.133\, H),$$

$$\frac{dB}{dt} = -\frac{1}{\tau}\, B,$$

$$\frac{dH}{dt} = -\frac{1}{\tau}\, H, \qquad G = \min\{0,\, -B,\, -H\}. \tag{7.21}$$

Two cases: $B \neq 0$, $H = 0$ and $B = 0$, $H \neq 0$ can be investigated separately. The eigenvalues of characteristic matrix are non-positive in both cases, so the exponential trajectory appears to be stable with respect to permutations of labour and energy.

7.4 Effect of Technological Shocks

Now, we again refer to the system of equations of economic growth 7.1 – 7.6 to consider a case, when the potential rates of production factors can be represented as a sum of the constant mean values and small time-dependent increments

$$\tilde{\delta} = \delta + \Delta\delta, \quad \tilde{\nu} = \nu + \Delta\nu, \quad \tilde{\eta} = \eta + \Delta\eta.$$

One can expect that in this case the trajectory of evolution would be close to the exponential one investigated in Section 7.2. Deviations of the trajectory from exponential one can be connected with changes of technology and investment. This phenomena can be described with tools we have developed already. We shall consider deviations from solution 7.8 – 7.10.

One can assume that investments and the technological coefficients can be taken in the form 7.17, that is

$$I = (\delta + \mu)(1 + G)K, \quad \lambda = \frac{\nu + \mu}{\delta + \mu}(1 + B)\frac{L}{K}, \quad \varepsilon = \frac{\eta + \mu}{\delta + \mu}(1 + H)\frac{E}{K}. \tag{7.22}$$

One can consider the quantities G, B, and H to be small ones, they are connected with the small increments of the rates of production factors according to equations 7.18.

To calculate the rate of the output growth close to an arbitrarily chosen initial moment of time, quantities $G(t)$, $B(t)$, and $H(t)$ can be approximated by linear functions

$$G(t) = G_0 + gt, \quad B(t) = B_0 + bt, \quad H(t) = H_0 + ht. \tag{7.23}$$

Now, one can use equations 7.3 to determine the growth rate of production factors

$$\frac{1}{L}\frac{dL}{dt} = \check{\nu} + (\nu + \mu)(b + g)t,$$

$$\frac{1}{E}\frac{dE}{dt} = \check{\eta} + (\eta + \mu)(h + g)t,$$

where

$$\check{\nu} = \nu + (\nu + \mu)(B_0 + G_0), \quad \check{\eta} = \eta + (\eta + \mu)(H_0 + G_0).$$

One can integrate these relations, to obtain trajectories of development

$$L = L_0 \exp\left(\breve{\nu}t + \frac{1}{2}(\nu + \mu)(b + g)t^2\right),$$

$$E = E_0 \exp\left(\breve{\eta}t + \frac{1}{2}(\eta + \mu)(h + g)t^2\right).$$

Now we can refer to formulae 6.19 to calculate the production of value and the rate of production growth

$$Y = Y_0\left[1 + \frac{1}{2}[(1 - \alpha)(\nu + \mu)(g + b)\right. \tag{7.24}$$

$$\left. +\alpha(\eta + \mu)(g + h)]\ t^2\ \frac{\nu + (q + \alpha)(\eta - \nu)}{\nu + \alpha(\eta - \nu)}\right]\ \exp\{[\breve{\nu} + (q + \alpha)(\breve{\eta} - \breve{\nu})]t\},$$

$$\frac{1}{Y}\frac{dY}{dt} = \breve{\nu} + (q + \alpha)(\breve{\eta} - \breve{\nu}) \tag{7.25}$$

$$+[(1 - \alpha)(\nu + \mu)(g + b) + \alpha(\eta + \mu)(g + h)]\ t\ \frac{\nu + (q + \alpha)(\eta - \nu)}{\nu + \alpha(\eta - \nu)}.$$

The above expression can be used for the assessment of effects of the technological coefficient variation and of investments on the increase in the rate of production of value at any moment of time.

When a decision is made to alter the rates of growth of the production factors, it is important to control variations of consumption level

$$w = \left(e^{q(\eta - \nu)t} - (\mu + \delta)\frac{K_0}{Y_0}\right)\frac{Y_0}{L_0}$$

$$\times \left(1 - \frac{K_0(\mu + \delta)g}{Y_0 - K_0(\mu + \delta)}t\right)\ \exp\{(\alpha + q)(\breve{\eta} - \breve{\nu})t\}. \tag{7.26}$$

Consumption level decreases with the increase of investments. From equation 7.26 at $g = 0$, one has consumption level 7.13 for the exponential growth.

7.5 Scenarios of Development

In this Section we shall apply the theory to the real development of the US economy to illustrate how the set of equations of growth works. To calculate GDP, one needs equations 7.1 – 7.6 for variables Y, K, L, $\tilde{L}$, E, I, $\bar{\lambda}$, $\bar{\varepsilon}$ and $\tilde{\delta}$, that is, the system of equations

$$\frac{dY}{dt} = \xi \left(I - \mu K\right), \quad \xi = Q \frac{L}{L_0 K} \left(\frac{EL_0}{E_0 L}\right)^{q+\alpha}, \quad \alpha = \frac{1 - \bar{\lambda}}{\bar{\varepsilon} - \bar{\lambda}},$$

$$\frac{dK}{dt} = I - \mu K, \quad \frac{dL}{dt} = \left(\bar{\lambda} \frac{I}{K} - \mu\right) L, \quad \frac{dE}{dt} = \left(\bar{\varepsilon} \frac{I}{K} - \mu\right) E,$$

$$\frac{I}{K} = \chi(u) + \min\left\{(\tilde{\delta} + \mu), \ (\tilde{\nu} + \mu)\frac{1}{\bar{\lambda}}, \ (\tilde{\eta} + \mu)\frac{1}{\bar{\varepsilon}}\right\},$$

$$\frac{d\bar{\lambda}}{dt} = -\frac{1}{\tau}\left(\bar{\lambda} - \frac{\tilde{\nu} + \mu}{\tilde{\delta} + \mu}\right), \quad \frac{d\bar{\varepsilon}}{dt} = -\frac{1}{\tau}\left(\bar{\varepsilon} - \frac{\tilde{\eta} + \mu}{\tilde{\delta} + \mu}\right),$$

$$\frac{d\tilde{\delta}}{dt} = -\frac{1}{\tau}\left(\tilde{\delta} - \tilde{\nu} - \alpha(\tilde{\eta} - \tilde{\nu})\right), \quad u = \frac{\tilde{L} - L}{\tilde{L}}, \quad \frac{d\tilde{L}}{dt} = \tilde{\nu}\tilde{L}. \quad (7.27)$$

One has to know share of governmental investment $\chi(u)$, which we consider to connected with unemployment u. We assume that it can be neglected here that is $\chi = 0$.

This system of equations 7.27 is a system of evolutionary equations, so that initial values of all variables have to be given. As initial year 1950 was chosen and initial values of variables in 1950 are used later.

Apart from that, one has to know parameters, characteristics of the production system, which are assumed to be constant: index of capital productivity growth $q = 0$; rate of depreciation $\mu = 0.05 \ year^{-1}$; time of technological rearrangement $\tau = 0.5 \ year$. One can see that a limited number of parameters ought to be given to characterise the internal state of production system, while some of these parameters can be considered as rather universal ones.

Scenarios of development can be obtained if one set potential rates of growth of labour and energy $\tilde{\nu}$ and $\tilde{\eta}$. Outputs of two scenarios of development of the US economy for years 1950 – 2090 are presented in Fig. 19. The initial values of parameters are chosen in such a way in order to reproduce the 'stylised' growth of quantities for years 1950 – 1990 (compare with curves in Figs 7 and 8). In both cases labour was taken as constant share of population, so $\tilde{\nu}$ coincides with rate of population growth, namely, $\tilde{\nu} = 0.01$ for the US. The first scenario corresponds to value $\tilde{\eta} = 0.0471$ for all years. The second one demonstrates diminishing supply of energy in the economy: the initial value of $\tilde{\eta} = 0.0471$ decreases to 0.03 in year 1990 and then to 0.01 in 2010. One can see that decrease in production consumption of energy leads to decrease of the rates of output.

To calculate the separate parts of national wealth, one can use equation 4.29 – 4.30 for value of stock of knowledge R

$$\frac{dR}{dt} = H - \mu R \qquad (7.28)$$

and equation 2.15 for value of residential wealth V, that is

$$\frac{dV}{dt} = J - \mu V, \qquad (7.29)$$

while one ought to know principles according to which the quantity

$$Y - I = J + H + \Pi$$

ought to be divided into three parts: investment in residential wealth J, investments in stock of knowledge H, and current consumption Π.

However, to calculate the total national wealth, one can use an equation for national wealth in the form

$$\frac{dW}{dt} = Y - w L - \mu K, \qquad (7.30)$$

where wage w can be calculated (see equation 6.33) as

$$w = \mu \frac{\bar{\varepsilon} - 1}{1 - \bar{\lambda}} \frac{K}{L}. \qquad (7.31)$$

Results of calculations of national wealth W in line with gross domestic product Y for the two above scenarios are shown in Fig 19.

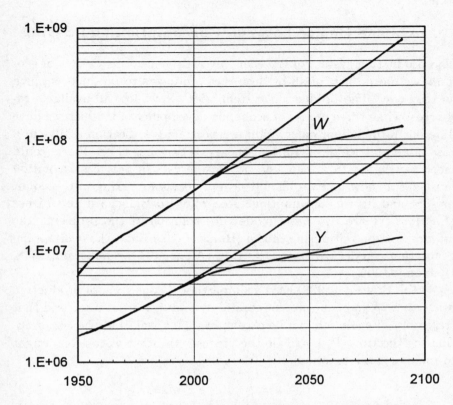

Figure 19 Output and national wealth in the US economy

However, these results ought to be considered as an illustration of the method of forecasting rather than forecast itself. One needs to know the future availability of labour and energy to do a real prediction.

One can see that the above system of equations permits us to draw scenarios of evolution of national economies for possible development of available production factors. However, as was already said in Section 7.1, the potential rates of growth ought to be considered as endogenous quantities in the problem of evolution of human population on the Earth (see Sections 4.4 and 4.5). These quantities can be calculated according to formulae 4.27 and 4.34, while one has to solve the problem of 'transformation of knowledge in energy'. We believe that after some research, one can formulate a more complete system of equations for variables N, W, Y, K, L, $\tilde{L}$, E, R, I, w, $\bar{\lambda}$, $\bar{\varepsilon}$ and $\tilde{\delta}$.

7.6   On the Choice between Consumption and Saving

The production system of the economy is driven by the desires of economic subjects, first of all by desires of producers to produce as much as they can. The production system tries to swallow all available resources, while three modes of economic development for which we have different formulae for calculation are possible (see Section 4.10). In a case of abundance of labour and energy, the desires of producers could meet restriction from the side of consumers. In this case a nation must decide how much it should save or consume, taking into account present and future consumption. According to Blanchard and Fisher (1989), there are two basic models for solution of the problem: the infinite horizon optimising model (Ramsay, 1928) and the overlapping generations model with finite horizon (Allais, 1947; Samuelson, 1958; Diamond, 1965).

Frank Ramsay (1928) used a simple model consisting of production function 1.23 and equation for capital dynamics 7.3. He supposed that trajectory of evolution can be chosen in such a way that the consumption for the time T should be the biggest. In other words, one ought to maximise the function

$$U(T) = \int_0^T u(c)\, e^{-\theta s}\, ds, \tag{7.32}$$

where consumption c is a function of the time s, $u(c)$ is a concave objective function, T is the horizon of planning.

We have no need to consider the original version of the Ramsay solution (it can be found, for example, in the monograph by Blanchard and Fisher, 1989); instead of it, we consider the problem as applying to evolution equations 7.1 – 7.3 which were formulated in Section 7.1. To introduce the consumption into equations, instead of relation 7.5, we take the relation

$$I = Y - cL$$

and rewrite equations 7.1 and 7.3 in the form

$$\frac{dY}{dt} = (\beta\lambda + \gamma\varepsilon)\, Y - (\beta\lambda + \gamma\varepsilon)\, cL - \mu\, (\beta\, L + \gamma\, E),$$

$$\frac{dK}{dt} = Y - cL - \mu\, K, \quad \frac{dL}{dt} = \lambda\, Y - (\lambda\, c + \mu)L, \quad \frac{dE}{dt} = \varepsilon\, Y - \varepsilon\, cL - \mu E. \tag{7.33}$$

Further on, it is convenient to use the variables

$$y = \frac{Y}{L}, \quad \epsilon = \frac{E}{L}, \quad \ell = \frac{L}{K}$$

to write down a system of evolutionary equations in the form

$$\frac{dy}{dt} = (\beta(\epsilon) - y)[\bar{\lambda}\,(y - c)\,\ell - \mu] + \gamma(\epsilon)[\bar{\epsilon}\,(y - c)\,\ell - \mu]\,\epsilon,$$

$$\frac{d\epsilon}{dt} = (\bar{\epsilon} - \bar{\lambda})\,(y - c)\,\epsilon\,\ell,$$

$$\frac{d\ell}{dt} = (\bar{\lambda} - 1)\,(y - c)\,\ell^2. \tag{7.34}$$

The technological variables $\bar{\lambda} = \lambda K/L$, $\bar{\epsilon} = \epsilon K/E$ are determined by equations 7.4. It is assumed that marginal productivities are given, for example, by formula 7.2.

One can use the standard procedure to find a trajectory which maximise function 7.32 under condition of restrictions 7.34. The result is a differential equation for consumption as function of time.

The second model – overlapping generation model – assumes that at any one time individuals of different generations are alive and may be interacting with one another. The investment is generated by individuals who save during their lives to ensure their consumption during retirement. In this way, preferences of individuals determine investment into production system.

It is clear that the discussed in this Section models can be very useful to estimate potential investment and potential rate of capital growth. However, it is necessary to take availability of labour and energy into account to obtain a real trajectory of evolution.

8 Multi-Sector Approach to Economic Growth

In this Chapter we return to the multi-sector model of production system, discussed in Chapter 3. We assume that production of value and dynamics of production factors in every sector are described in the same way as for the whole economy. It allows us to include technological changes and restrictions imposed by availability of labour and energy into consideration. The system is assumed to be characterised by the fundamental matrices A and B introduced in Section 3.1. In fact, the components of matrices enter in equations in a unique combination forming the capital marginal productivity matrix Ξ which itself ought to be considered as characteristic of the production system. Apart from it, coefficient of amortisation μ and times of rearrangement of production equipment τ^i, as constants parameters, have to be given. To design the scenarios of development, the potential rates of growth of labour and energy in every sector $\tilde{\nu}^i(t)$ and $\tilde{\eta}^i(t)$, as functions of time, have to be assumed. They relate apparently to potential rates of production factors growth for the whole economy. Now we are in position to draw a detailed picture of economic growth, taking into account specialisation of each sector.

8.1 Sectoral Investments

To calculate the sectoral final output Y_j, $j = 1, 2, \ldots n$, one can start with equations 3.48, that is

$$\frac{dY_j}{dt} = \sum_{i=1}^{n} \xi_j^i \left(\Gamma^i - \mu K^i \right), \quad j = 1, 2, \ldots n, \tag{8.1}$$

$$\frac{dK^i}{dt} = \Gamma^i - \mu K^i, \quad i = 1, 2, \ldots n. \tag{8.2}$$

The capital marginal productivities ξ_j^i were defined in Section 3.5

through components of the fundamental technological matrices as

$$\xi_j^i = \frac{\delta_j^i - a_j^i}{b^i}, \quad j, i = 1, 2, \ldots n.$$

The capital marginal productivity ξ_j^i shows how an increase in production equipment in sector i affects final output of product j. An example of capital marginal productivity matrix can be found in Section 3.5.

The rates of growth of the production factors are defined by equations 4.14 which can be rewritten as

$$\frac{dL^i}{dt} = \lambda^i I^i - \mu L^i, \quad \frac{dE^i}{dt} = \varepsilon^i I^i - \mu E^i. \tag{8.3}$$

Sectoral technological coefficients λ^i and ε^i ($i = 1, 2, \ldots, n$) characterise a level of applied technology. One can assume that the dimensionless technological variables

$$\bar{\lambda}^i = \lambda^i K^i / L^i, \qquad \bar{\varepsilon}^i = \varepsilon^i K^i / E^i$$

are determined by equations 4.40 and 4.41 for each sector, that is,

$$\frac{d\bar{\lambda}^i}{dt} = -\frac{1}{\tau^i} \left(\bar{\lambda}^i - \frac{\tilde{\nu}^i + \mu}{\tilde{\delta}^i + \mu} \right), \quad \frac{d\bar{\varepsilon}^i}{dt} = -\frac{1}{\tau^i} \left(\bar{\varepsilon}^i - \frac{\tilde{\eta}^i + \mu}{\tilde{\delta}^i + \mu} \right). \tag{8.4}$$

Time of crossover τ^i from one technological situation to another can be different for different sectors. It is determined by internal processes of substitution of technology in sector.

To determine sectoral investments I^i in equations 8.1, 8.2 and 8.3, one has to take into account internal and external restrictions on the development of the system. The internal restriction are imposed by limiting output of the production system and by necessary consumption. These restrictions determine potential sectoral investments $\tilde{I}^i$ which are connected with potential rate of sectoral capital growth $\tilde{\delta}^i$

$$\tilde{I}^i = (\tilde{\delta}^i + \mu) K^i. \tag{8.5}$$

It is assumed that there is a method, for example, the method described in Section 3.5 to calculate potential sectoral investments and, consequently, according to relation 8.5 the potential rate of capital growth.

We follow the discussion of Chapter 4 to assert that external restrictions are imposed by availability of labour and energy which is given for every sector by their potential rates of growth $\tilde{\nu}^i(t)$ and $\tilde{\eta}^i(t)$. These exogenous characteristics are considered to be functions of time.

Then, we can assume that relation 4.37 is valid for each sector, so one has

$$I^i = \chi^i K + \min\left\{\tilde{I}^i, \ (\tilde{\nu}^i + \mu)L^i/\lambda^i, \ (\tilde{\eta}^i + \mu)E^i/\varepsilon^i\right\}, \qquad (8.6)$$

where χ^i is governmental intervention in sector i.

By relation 8.6, three modes of development of each sector are determined. The first line in relation 8.6 corresponds to the internal restrictions. The middle equation in 8.6 is valid in the case of abundance of energy and raw materials and a lack of labour. In this case, labour is used completely and there is a possibility for attracting extra energy. The latter is a reason for technological changes. Internal processes lead to decrease of labour and increase of energy in production processes. The lower equation is valid in the case of lack of energy and abundance of labour and raw materials. However, there are many sectors each of which can work in one of the three modes. So, there are many possible modes of development of a multi-sector economy.

We assume here that there is no restriction due to material resources.

8.2 Sectoral Marginal Productivities

On the basis of relations 3.2 and 3.8, increase in production of value in every sector Z^i $(i = 1, 2, .., n)$ is connected with increase in amount of sectoral production equipment or sectoral capital K^i

$$\frac{dZ^i}{dt} = \xi^i \frac{dK^i}{dt}, \quad \xi^i = \sum_{j=1}^{n} \xi_j^i. \qquad (8.7)$$

From the other side, production of value is determined by consumed labour and energy. So, relation 6.4 for production of value can be written for every sector

$$\frac{dZ^i}{dt} = \beta_i \frac{dL^i}{dt} + \gamma_i \frac{dE^i}{dt}, \qquad (8.8)$$

where L^i and E^i are labour and energy consumed in sector i. Sectoral marginal productivities of production factors, β_i and γ_i are introduced here. One can imagine that the productivities of a sector depend, generally speaking, on the production factors consumed in the all other sectors.[1] However, we use the simplest assumption that the sectoral marginal productivities are determined by the production factors consumed in this sector only. In this case, on the analogy of formulae 6.15, approximate formulae can be written for productivities

$$\beta_i = Q^i \frac{1 - \alpha^i}{L_0^i} (\Xi^i)^{q^i + \alpha^i}, \qquad \gamma_i = Q^i \frac{\alpha^i}{E_0^i} (\Xi^i)^{q^i + \alpha^i - 1}. \qquad (8.9)$$

The sectoral marginal productivity β_i and γ_i depend on the production factors taken in combination

$$\Xi^i = \frac{L_0^i}{L^i} \frac{E^i}{E_0^i}.$$

Then, we can use equations 8.2 and 8.3, to rewrite equations 8.7 and 8.8 in the form

$$\frac{dZ^i}{dt} = \xi^i (I^i - \mu K^i), \qquad \frac{dZ^i}{dt} = (\beta_i \lambda^i + \gamma_i \varepsilon^i) I^i - \mu (\beta_i L^i + \gamma_i E^i).$$
$$(8.10)$$

Further on, to determine the relation between the marginal productivities, we refer to the procedure which was used in Section 6.3. First, we compare equations 8.10 to find the relation between characteristic parameters of the system

$$\beta_i \lambda^i + \gamma_i \varepsilon^i = \xi^i,$$
$$\beta_i L^i + \gamma_i E^i = \xi^i K^i.$$

---

[1]It is possible to expect that quantities of marginal productivities are determined by mutual market of production factors. So we can believe that productivities of a sector depend on the sums of production factors and are expressed by the same formula, so we can write down for each sector

$$\beta_i = Q^i \frac{1 - \alpha}{L_0} \Xi^{q + \alpha}, \quad \gamma_i = Q^i \frac{\alpha}{E_0} \Xi^{q + \alpha - 1}, \quad \Xi = \frac{L_0}{L} \frac{E}{E_0}.$$

The latter relations can be considered to be a set of equations for the marginal productivities; so, one can find

$$\beta_i = \xi^i \, \frac{\bar{\varepsilon}^i - 1}{\bar{\varepsilon}^i - \bar{\lambda}^i} \, \frac{K^i}{L^i}, \qquad \gamma_i = \xi^i \, \frac{1 - \bar{\lambda}^i}{\bar{\varepsilon}^i - \bar{\lambda}^i} \, \frac{K^i}{E^i}. \qquad (8.11)$$

From the other side, these quantities are expressed by relations 8.9, so that one can obtain

$$\xi^i = Q^i \, \frac{L^i}{L_0^i K^i} \left(\Xi^i \right)^{q^i + \alpha^i}, \qquad \alpha^i = \frac{1 - \bar{\lambda}^i}{\bar{\varepsilon}^i - \bar{\lambda}^i}. \qquad (8.12)$$

The constant Q^i is determined by initial values of variables. The sense of the parameters q^i is defined by an equation of the kind of 6.27. We consider them to be given parameters.

Now, we can use equations 3.7 and 3.8 which can be written in the form

$$\frac{dX_i}{dt} = \frac{1}{1 - a^i} \frac{dZ^i}{dt}, \qquad \frac{dY_j}{dt} = \sum_{i=1}^{n} \frac{\delta_j^i - a_j^i}{1 - a^i} \frac{dZ^i}{dt}.$$

Then, expressions 8.10 for the sectoral production of value determine the dynamics of sectoral outputs: gross output X_j and final output Y_j

$$\frac{dX_i}{dt} = \frac{1}{1 - a^i}(\beta_i \lambda^i + \gamma_i \varepsilon^i)(I^i - \breve{I}^i) = \frac{1}{b^i} \, (I^i - \breve{I}^i), \qquad (8.13)$$

$$\frac{dY_j}{dt} = \sum_{i=1}^{n} (\xi_j^i / \xi^i) \, (\beta_i \lambda^i + \gamma_i \varepsilon^i)(I^i - \breve{I}^i) = \sum_{i=1}^{n} \xi_j^i (I^i - \breve{I}^i), \qquad (8.14)$$

where sectoral investments of the zeroth growth are introduced

$$\breve{I}^i = \mu \, \frac{\beta_i \, L^i + \gamma_i \, E^i}{\beta_i \, \lambda^i + \gamma_i \, \varepsilon^i} = \mu \, K^{\cdot i}. \qquad (8.15)$$

One can see from relation 8.14 that all the components of the matrix of capital marginal productivity are needed to calculate the final product, so that one needs to know the approximation for the components which can be expressed through components of the input-output matrix

$$\xi_j^i = \xi^i \, \frac{\delta_j^i - a_j^i}{1 - a^i}, \qquad (8.16)$$

where ξ^i is defined by equation 8.12.

Let us note, that relations 8.7 and 8.8 are valid for the case, when all prices of products do not depend on time. In the opposite case, we ought to use a new quantity $\hat{Z}^i$, namely, production of value measured in current money unit, for which we have

$$\frac{d\hat{Z}^i}{dt} = p_i \left(\frac{dZ^i}{dt} \right)_{p_i} + \hat{Z}^i \frac{d\ln p_i}{dt}, \qquad (8.17)$$

where $\left(\dfrac{dZ^i}{dt} \right)_{p_i}$ is production of value in sector i at constant prices given by formula 8.7 or 8.8.

Index of price of the product p_i must be considered to be a new variable. One needs extra equations to include them into consideration in this case. Some equations were discussed in Chapter 5. Further on, we restrict ourselves to the case when all prices are constant.

8.3 Exponential Growth and Rules of Aggregation

We consider a simple case, when rates of growth of production factors are constant but, generally speaking different for different sectors, that is

$$\tilde{\delta}^i = \delta^i, \quad \tilde{\nu}^i = \nu^i, \quad \tilde{\eta}^i = \eta^i.$$

In this case, we use the solution of equations 8.2 – 8.6 in the form

$$\Gamma^i = (\delta^i + \mu)K^i, \qquad \lambda^i = \frac{\nu^i + \mu}{\delta^i + \mu} \frac{L^i}{K^i}, \qquad \varepsilon^i = \frac{\eta^i + \mu}{\delta^i + \mu} \frac{E^i}{K^i}, \qquad (8.18)$$

$$K^i = K_0^i \exp \delta^i t, \qquad L^i = L_0^i \exp \nu^i t, \qquad E^i = E_0^i \exp \eta^i t. \qquad (8.19)$$

Then, we use expressions 8.10 and 8.12, to obtain the expression for sectoral production of value

$$Z^i = Z_0^i \exp \left[\nu^i + (q^i + \alpha^i)(\eta^i - \nu^i) \right]t = Z_0^i \exp \left[\delta^i + q^i(\eta^i - \nu^i) \right]t, \qquad (8.20)$$

where

$$Z_0^i = \frac{\delta^i}{\delta^i + q^i(\eta^i - \nu^i)} Q^i. \qquad (8.21)$$

Referring to natural definition of aggregate production factors discussed in Sections 2.4 (equation 2.25) and 4.2 (equation 4.5), one can return to description of the production system as a whole. It is convenient to introduce mean rates of growth of production factors by relations

$$\delta = \frac{1}{K_0} \sum_{i=1}^{n} \delta^i K_0^i, \quad \nu = \frac{1}{L_0} \sum_{i=1}^{n} \nu^i L_0^i, \quad \eta = \frac{1}{E_0} \sum_{i=1}^{n} \eta^i E_0^i. \qquad (8.22)$$

We shall consider the case when quantities $(\delta^i - \delta)t$, $(\nu^i - \nu)t$, and $(\eta^i - \eta)t$ are small. So, retaining only the first terms with respect to these small quantities one has, to a good approximation,

$$K = K_0 e^{\delta t}, \qquad L = L_0 e^{\nu t}, \qquad E = E_0 e^{\eta t}. \qquad (8.23)$$

Then, we use formulae 2.22 and 4.16 to obtain

$$I = (\delta + \mu)(1 + gt)K, \quad g = \frac{1}{\delta + \mu} \sum_{i=1}^{n} (\delta^i - \delta)^2 \frac{K_0^i}{K_0}, \qquad (8.24)$$

$$\lambda = \frac{\nu + \mu}{\delta + \mu}(1 + bt)\frac{L}{K}, \quad b = -g + \frac{1}{\nu + \mu} \sum_{i=1}^{n} (\nu^i - \nu)^2 \frac{L_0^i}{L_0}, \quad (8.25)$$

$$\varepsilon = \frac{\eta + \mu}{\delta + \mu}(1 + ht)\frac{E}{K}, \quad h = -g + \frac{1}{\eta + \mu} \sum_{i=1}^{n} (\eta^i - \eta)^2 \frac{E_0^i}{E_0}. \quad (8.26)$$

Relations 8.24 – 8.26 have a form of relations 7.22 – 7.23, while the additives are seen to be connected with the difference of the rates of growth of production factors in sectors.

Then, one can estimate the rate of growth of the final output which according to equation 8.14 can be written as

$$\frac{dY}{dt} = \sum_{i=1}^{n} \xi^i \left(I^i - \mu K^i \right), \qquad (8.27)$$

where capital marginal productivity ξ^i is defined by relation 8.12 and for the considered case of constant sectoral rates of growth of production factors can be written with the help of relation 8.19 in a form

$$\xi^i = \frac{Z_0^i}{K_0^i} \frac{1}{\delta^i} \left(\delta^i + q^i (\eta^i - \nu^i) \right) \exp \left(q^i (\eta^i - \nu^i) t \right). \qquad (8.28)$$

Time dependence of marginal productivities is connected with parameters q^i that is, eventually with time dependence of components of the fundamental technological matrices.

One can use the expression for sectoral investment from relations 8.18, so that equation 8.27 can be rewritten as

$$\frac{dY}{dt} = \sum_{i=1}^{n} Z_0^i \left(\delta^i + q^i \left(\eta^i - \nu^i \right) \right) \exp \left(\delta^i + q^i \left(\eta^i - \nu^i \right) \right) t. \qquad (8.29)$$

Then, the time dependence of the final output can be found. We need to integrate equation 8.29 to obtain final output as a function of time

$$Y = \sum_{i=1}^{n} Z_0^i \exp \left(\delta^i + q^i \left(\eta^i - \nu^i \right) \right) t. \qquad (8.30)$$

To estimate the rate of growth, we take the zeroth terms of expansion of quantities 8.29 and 8.30 with respect to small quantities connected with time from initial moment $t = 0$. So, one can obtain an approximate expression for the rate of growth of output

$$\frac{1}{Y} \frac{dY}{dt} = \delta + \frac{1}{Y_0} \sum_{i=1}^{n} Z_0^i \left(\delta^i - \delta + q^i (\eta^i - \nu^i) \right). \qquad (8.31)$$

Deviations of rate of growth of final output from rate of capital growth δ can be connected first of all with non-homogeneity of sectoral development and then with change of productivity. Let me remind the reader that quantities q^i are connected with capital marginal productivities ξ^i which, in their turn, are determined by components of fundamental technological matrices that is, the quantities are determined by applied technology. Relation 8.31 explains why the rate of output growth can be close to one of capital and reveals reasons of observed deviations.

8.4 Equations of Economic Growth

Now, one can collect all previous results to write down a closed set of equations for the dynamics of the production system, which is assumed to consist of n sectors. The equations can be written in different equivalent forms, by making use of different sets of variables. Here, we assume that every sector (labelled i, $i = 1, 2, \ldots, n$) is described by variables:

Y_i – final output,
K^i – value of production equipment,
L^i – consumption of labour,
E^i – consumption of energy,
I^i – real investment,
$\tilde{I}^i$ – potential investment,
$\bar{\lambda}^i$ – labour requirement,
$\bar{\varepsilon}^i$ – energy requirement.[1]

We refer to previous results of this Chapter and Chapter 3 to collect the set of equations for listed variables:

$$\frac{dY_j}{dt} = \sum_{i=1}^{n} \xi^i \frac{\delta_j^i - a_j^i}{1 - a^i} (I^i - \mu K^i),$$

$$\xi^i = Q^i \frac{L^i}{L_0^i K^i} \left(\frac{L_0^i}{L^i} \frac{E^i}{E_0^i} \right)^{q^i + \alpha^i}, \quad \alpha^i = \frac{1 - \bar{\lambda}^i}{\bar{\varepsilon}^i - \bar{\lambda}^i},$$

$$\frac{dK^i}{dt} = I^i - \mu K^i, \quad \frac{dL^i}{dt} = \left(\bar{\lambda}^i \frac{I^i}{K^i} - \mu \right) L^i, \quad \frac{dE^i}{dt} = \left(\bar{\varepsilon}^i \frac{I^i}{K^i} - \mu \right) E^i,$$

$$\frac{I^i}{K^i} = \chi^i + \min \left\{ \frac{\tilde{I}^i}{K^i}, \ (\tilde{\nu}^i + \mu) \frac{1}{\bar{\lambda}^i}, \ (\tilde{\eta}^i + \mu) \frac{1}{\bar{\varepsilon}^i} \right\},$$

$$\frac{d\bar{\lambda}^i}{dt} = -\frac{1}{\tau^i} \left(\bar{\lambda}^i - (\tilde{\nu}^i + \mu) \frac{K^i}{\tilde{I}^i} \right), \quad \frac{d\bar{\varepsilon}^i}{dt} = -\frac{1}{\tau^i} \left(\bar{\varepsilon}^i - (\tilde{\eta}^i + \mu) \frac{K^i}{\tilde{I}^i} \right),$$

$$\max \sum_{i=1}^{n} \xi^i (\tilde{I}^i - \mu K^i), \quad \sum_{i=1}^{n} \tilde{I}^i \leq \sum_{j=1}^{n} \left(Y_j - w_j \sum_{k=1}^{n} L^k \right). \tag{8.32}$$

---

[1]For example, the sectoral production of value Z^i and the gross output X_i can be added to the list of variables as well. In this case the set of equations ought to be completed by equations 8.10 and 8.13.

This is a set of evolutionary equations, so that initial values of the variables, that is,

$$Y_i(0), \quad K^i(0), \quad L^i(0), \quad E^i(0), \quad I^i(0), \quad \tilde{I}^i(0), \quad \bar{\lambda}^i(0), \quad \bar{\varepsilon}^i(0)$$

ought to be given. It is assumed that potential sectoral investments $\tilde{I}^i$ are defined here as investment of the fastest growth for the case when there is abundance of labour and energy, that is, the investment are calculated with method described in Section 3.5. The problem, in this case one has Cauchy problem, can be solved by numerical methods, while the optimisation problem ought to be solved at every step of the solution. The equations determine a trajectory of evolution of the production system. The final consumption and the storage of intermediate products appear to be the consequence of evolution of the system.

We list below what parameters have to be known for solution of the above system of equations:

a^i_j – fundamental technological matrix – input-output matrix defined by relation 3.1. Components of the matrix ought to be found empirically and to be given as functions of time.

q^i – index of capital productivity growth in sector i. It is usually a small quantity, so that at the start it can be equated to zero.

μ – coefficient of depreciation of production equipment. It is a simplification that it is constant quantity taken as the same for all products in all situations.

τ^i – times of rearrangement (diffusion) of production technology have to be given as constant parameters.

χ^i – governmental intervention in sector i. It ought to be switched on when there is a need to diminish a gap between proposed and real consumption of production factors (to diminish unemployment, for example).

w_j – the lowest level of consumption of product j per labour unit.

$\tilde{\nu}^i$ – potential rate of growth of labour in every sector ought to be given as a function of time.

$\tilde{\eta}^i$ – potential rate of growth of energy in every sector ought to be given as a function of time.

The parameters a^i_j and q^i are connected with the matrix of capital marginal productivities ξ^i_j defined by equation 8.16. It is a fundamental characteristic of production system. The quantities ξ^i_j, μ and τ^i are internal technological characteristics of production system. These quantities are determined by applied technology and one can say that the technology in input-output model is given, if one knows these parameters. Potential rates of growth of the production factors $\tilde{\nu}^i(t)$ and $\tilde{\eta}^i(t)$ ought to be considered as characteristics of technology as well, but, in contrast to above characteristics, these quantities are characteristics of possible technology.

Note that the above system of equations are valid for the case when all prices or, in other words, money unit to measure value, are considered to be constant during the time. The system can be reformulated for the case when prices change. In this case one has to introduce the new variables for the final output measured in current money unit $\hat{Y}_i$ instead of variables Y_i (using equation 8.17). Some equations for indexes of prices of the product p_i, $i = 1, 2, \ldots, n$, which must be considered to be new variables, have to be added as well. Some principles of the design of equations for price indices were discussed in Chapter 5.

We think that the equations reflect some universal features of production systems. In our theory, economic growth is coupled with growth of consumed energy and technological changes. Understanding of the energy-economy coupling in production system was considered to be crucial for design of proper models for generating scenarios of development and much effort and money was spent to create a few different simulation models of energy-economy system (Shapot *et al*, 1995; Wene, 1996). Such models provide us with many details of internal processes but require much input information (many empirical parameters). In contrast to it, phenomenological models, such as above, looks simpler and deal with aggregate variables. They can be helpful to draw up reliable scenarios of evolution of global and national economies in macroeconomic terms for governments and banks.

Appendix Data on the US Economy

Time series on an annual basis provide the basic empirical data for the test of each theory of economic growth. National statistical compilations contain information about gross national product, labour, energy, and other quantities. The series that follow are based on the series of relative quantities compiled by Scott (1989). Data taken from International Financial Statistics Yearbook (1997), from Brown (1966) and from Historical Statistics (1975) are used to restore absolute values of gross national product Y, gross investment I and used labour L. The amount of available production capital K is calculated according to equation 2.13 at $\mu = 0.05$. Capital series apparently depends on value of depreciation coefficient μ which, generally speaking, is not constant.[1] The initial data for consumption of energy E are taken from Energy Statistics Yearbook (1995) for recent years and from Historical Statistics (1975) for earlier years. The quantity shown in Table represents production consumption of energy which assumes to increase in previous years at a rate of 15% and was about 70% in 1995.

High art and hard work are needed to find time series for economic quantities.[2] The series depend on methods of estimation, so that there might be some discrepancies in series from different sources. We do not discuss discrepancies here, for we use the series not for analysis of economic growth but only for illustration of methods of analysis.

---

[1] Ayres (1997a) estimates that rate of capital depreciation μ was 0.03 in 1909, had increased to 0.05 by 1949 and it is greater (0.06 - 0.08) at the moment. We have to use constant value, so as our equations are simplified at this assumption. However, there is no difficulty to write equations for more realistic case.

[2] Sometimes, it needs for courage as well. It was very dangerous work for researches in USSR to collect numbers. Joseph Stalin did not like 'games in digits'. Russian economist Kondratiev died in prison trying to understand how economy was going. From prison, he sent a letter with ideas about the theory of economic growth (Kondratiev, 1989).

Year	Population $N \cdot 10^{-6}$	GNP $Y \cdot 10^{-6}$ $ (1990)	Investment $I \cdot 10^{-6}$ $ (1990)	Capital $K \cdot 10^{-6}$ $ (1990)	Labour $L \cdot 10^{-6}$ man-hour	Energy $E \cdot 10^{-6}$ t.c.e.
1896	–	291,663	49,965	324,000	40,471	30
1897	–	322,919	60,678	357,765	42,088	34
1898	–	329,446	56,654	400,554	42,605	37
1899	–	369,384	71,259	437,180	45,986	40
1900	76.09	372,917	80,521	486,581	47,057	43
1901	77.58	414,712	89,638	542,773	49,745	57
1902	79.16	411,239	93,557	605,272	52,831	75
1903	80.63	429,801	92,409	668,565	54,936	79
1904	82.17	421,538	76,840	727,546	54,914	80
1905	83.82	457,464	82,975	768,009	58,266	71
1906	85.45	521,294	111,249	812,584	61,338	79
1907	87.01	525,784	109,745	883,204	63,250	88
1908	88.71	468,781	68,555	948,789	61,648	96
1909	90.49	536,203	108,914	969,904	65,761	93
1910	92.41	535,245	107,674	1,030,323	68,027	99
1911	93.86	553,148	94,625	1,086,481	69,571	105
1912	95.36	575,722	111,144	1,126,782	72,295	114
1913	97.23	598,775	123,889	1,181,587	73,839	103
1914	99.11	539,856	66,285	1,246,397	72,960	112
1915	100.55	557,280	63,581	1,250,362	73,551	114
1916	101.96	650,270	107,529	1,251,424	79,819	127
1917	103.27	620,930	85,337	1,296,382	81,887	141
1918	103.21	657,455	78,463	1,316,900	82,256	157
1919	104.51	695,178	131,898	1,329,518	82,552	163
1920	106.46	710,746	178,287	1,394,940	83,142	153
1921	108.54	668,233	74,096	1,503,479	77,678	153
1922	110.05	702,962	92,910	1,502,401	83,511	149
1923	111.95	813,137	153,351	1,520,191	90,821	158
1924	114.11	838,884	98,399	1,597,532	89,271	164
1925	115.83	852,057	144,009	1,616,055	92,594	174
1926	117.40	913,731	154,235	1,679,261	96,359	169
1927	119.04	919,120	136,212	1,749,533	97,172	184
1928	120.51	986,781	133,468	1,798,268	98,648	200
1929	121.77	993,967	170,845	1,841,822	101,897	208
1930	123.08	888,582	113,677	1,920,577	96,433	201

	$N \cdot 10^{-6}$	$Y \cdot 10^{-6}$ $ (1990)	$I \cdot 10^{-6}$ $ (1990)	$K \cdot 10^{-6}$ $ (1990)	$L \cdot 10^{-6}$ man-hour	$E \cdot 10^{-6}$ t.c.e.
1931	124.04	794,575	61,100	1,938,225	88,459	186
1932	124.84	658,054	1,794	1,902,414	79,376	169
1933	125.58	637,097	15,740	1,809,087	79,819	175
1934	126.37	689,190	42,352	1,734,373	83,364	178
1935	127.25	771,821	87,791	1,690,006	88,089	185
1936	128.05	864,631	113,783	1,693,297	96,138	192
1937	128.82	955,645	159,222	1,722,415	101,897	195
1938	129.82	868,823	71,879	1,795,516	94,883	212
1939	130.88	952,651	103,676	1,777,619	100,864	231
1940	132.12	1,050,850	156,807	1,792,415	106,771	251
1941	133.40	1,246,650	207,577	1,859,601	121,022	273
1942	134.86	1,393,948	100,655	1,974,198	130,916	297
1943	136.74	1,492,746	52,102	1,976,143	136,823	323
1944	138.40	1,529,272	67,552	1,929,438	134,830	351
1945	139.93	1,487,956	103,689	1,900,518	129,882	353
1946	141.39	1,453,227	241,142	1,909,181	136,528	354
1947	144.13	1,474,783	206,073	2,054,864	142,583	368
1948	146.63	1,599,927	271,711	2,158,193	144,724	382
1949	149.19	1,547,235	183,789	2,321,995	138,595	401
1950	152.27	1,717,886	294,893	2,389,684	143,912	413
1951	154.88	1,835,844	336,150	2,565,093	153,585	460
1952	157.55	1,880,154	274,324	2,772,988	157,720	464
1953	160.18	1,953,803	274,786	2,908,662	161,928	483
1954	163.03	1,913,086	250,892	3,038,015	155,947	476
1955	165.93	2,083,737	343,380	3,137,006	161,928	530
1956	168.90	2,147,208	366,614	3,323,535	165,768	560
1957	171.98	2,160,381	349,093	3,523,972	165,399	569
1958	174.88	2,103,497	283,084	3,696,866	159,344	575
1959	177.83	2,266,364	359,991	3,795,107	166,285	609
1960	180.67	2,283,728	352,035	3,965,343	167,245	643
1961	183.69	2,311,272	338,287	4,119,110	166,728	662
1962	186.54	2,437,015	385,982	4,251,442	171,011	703
1963	189.24	2,533,417	397,487	4,424,852	174,038	742
1964	191.89	2,681,914	431,527	4,601,097	178,099	787
1965	194.30	2,868,133	526,469	4,802,569	185,040	833
1966	196.56	3,033,993	598,586	5,088,909	192,572	894
1967	198.71	3,091,476	509,319	5,433,050	195,377	938
1968	200.71	3,244,762	575,362	5,670,716	200,472	1,009
1969	202.68	3,340,566	602,414	5,962,543	205,493	1,077
1970	205.05	3,294,461	577,451	6,266,829	203,574	1,133

	$N \cdot 10^{-6}$	$Y \cdot 10^{-6}$ $\$ (1990)$	$I \cdot 10^{-6}$ $\$ (1990)$	$K \cdot 10^{-6}$ $\$ (1990)$	$L \cdot 10^{-6}$ man-hour	$E \cdot 10^{-6}$ t.c.e.
1971	207.66	3,391,462	613,665	6,530,939	203,500	1,176
1972	209.90	3,618,398	680,473	6,818,057	209,924	1,251
1973	211.91	3,859,704	730,919	7,157,627	220,040	1,323
1974	213.85	3,786,654	704,604	7,530,665	221,738	1,310
1975	215.97	3,747,135	651,163	7,858,735	215,314	1,292
1976	218.04	3,969,280	696,499	8,116,961	222,181	1,382
1977	220.24	4,210,587	785,832	8,407,612	230,820	1,420
1978	222.58	4,488,418	872,571	8,773,063	242,634	1,454
1979	225.06	4,587,216	920,979	9,206,981	251,717	1,502
1980	227.22	4,522,548	872,045	9,667,611	250,757	1,463
1981	229.47	4,633,322	876,017	10,056,275	254,523	1,440
1982	231.66	4,469,257	807,787	10,429,479	249,575	1,395
1983	233.79	4,611,766	826,047	10,715,792	257,328	1,404
1984	235.82	4,972,827	913,141	11,006,049	274,828	1,482
1985	237.92	5,105,157	944,699	11,368,888	283,541	1,519
1986	240.13	5,186,800	964,009	11,745,143	289,365	1,538
1987	242.29	5,346,400	948,519	12,121,895	294,353	1,610
1988	244.50	5,556,700	958,526	12,464,320	298,783	1,720
1989	246.82	5,697,400	963,770	12,799,629	304,188	1,766
1990	249.44	5,743,800	927,700	13,123,418	306,442	1,780
1991	252.12	5,687,900	838,558	13,394,947	307,707	1,969
1992	255.00	5,842,700	881,197	13,563,757	311,830	2,025
1993	257.75	5,973,100	950,775	13,766,766	314,428	2,092
1994	260.29	6,183,600	1,026,827	14,029,203	321,837	2,169
1995	262.76	6,309,100	1,073,391	14,354,570	324,899	2,241
1996	265.18	6,462,500	1,121,331	14,710,233	328,929	2,351
1997	267.64	6,714,600	1,233,464	15,096,053	331,561	2,395

Bibliography

Adams, J.D. (1990), 'Fundamental Stocks of Knowledge and Productivity Growth', *Journal of Political Economy*, vol. 98 (4), pp. 673-702.

Afriat, S.N. (1977), *The Price Index*, Cambridge University Press, Cambridge *etc.*

Allais, M. (1947), *Economie et interet*, Imprimerie Nationale, Paris.

Allen, E.L (1979), *Energy and Economic Growth in the United States*, MIT Press, Cambridge MA.

Allen, R.G.D. (1963), *Mathematical Economics, 2nd Ed.*, Macmillan, London.

Arrow, K.J. and Debreu, G. (1954), 'Existence of an Equilibrium for a Competitive Economy', *Econometrica*, vol. 22 (3), pp. 265-290.

Ayres, R.U. (1989), 'The Future of Technological Forecasting', *Technological Forecasting and Social Change*, vol. 36 (1), pp. 49-60.

Ayres, R.U. (1997 a), *Theories of Economic Growth*, Working Paper 97/13/EPS, INSEAD, Fontainebleau, France.

Ayres, R.U. (1997 b), 'Comments on Georgescu-Roegen', *Ecological Economics*, vol. 22, pp. 285-287.

Ayres, R.U. (1998 a), *The Second Law, the Fourth Law, Recycling and Limits to Growth*, Working Paper 98/38/CMER, INSEAD, Fontainebleau, France.

Ayres, R.U. (1998 b), *Theoretical Growth Models vs Real World Evidence: Implication for Greenhouse Gas Policy*, Working paper 98/63/EPS, INSEAD, Fontainebleau, France.

Ayres, R.U. (1998 c), 'Technological Progress: A Proposed Measure', *Technological Forecasting and Social Change*, vol. 59, pp. 213-233 .

Barlow, R. (1994), 'Population Growth and Economic Growth: Some More Correlation', *Population and Development Review*, vol. 20 (1), pp. 153-165.

Baumol, W.J. (1977), *Economic Theory and Operations Analysis, 4th Ed*, Prentice-Hall, London.

Berndt, E. R. and Wood, D.O. (1979), 'Engineering and Econometric Interpretations of Energy – Capital Complementarity', *American Economic Review*, vol. 69, pp. 342-354.

Blanchard, O.J. and Fisher, S. (1989), *Lectures on Macroeconomics*, MIT Press, Gambridge MA.

Blanchflower, D.G. and Oswald, A.J. (1994), *The Wage Curve*, MIT Press, Cambridge MA and London.

Blaug, M. (1997), *Economic Theory in Retrospect, 5th Ed*, Cambridge University Press, Cambridge *etc.*

Blaug, M. (1998), 'Disturbing Currents in Modern Economics', *Challenge*, vol. 41 (3), pp. 11 - 34.

Brown, M. (1966), *On the Theory and Measurement of Technological Change*, Cambridge University Press, Cambridge.

Callen, H.B. (1960), *Thermodynamics and an Introduction to Thermostatics*, Wiley, New York.

Carr-Saunders, A.M. (1936), *World Population: Past Growth and Present Trends*, Oxford University Press, London.

Cheremnykh, Yu.N. (1982), *Analiz povedenija trajectorii dinamiki narodnokhozjaistvennykh modelei, in Russian (Analysis of Trajectories of Economical Models)*, Nauka, Moscow.

Ciaschini, M. (1993), *Modelling the Structure of the Economy*, Chapman and Hall, London *etc.*

Clark C. (1968), *Population Growth and Land Use*, Macmillan, London *etc.*

Cleveland, C.J., Costanza, R., Hall, Ch.A.S. and Kaufmann, R. (1984), 'Energy and the U.S. Economy: A Biophysical Perspective', *Science*, vol. 225, pp. 890-897.

Cobb, G.W. and Douglas, P.N. (1928), 'A Theory of Production', *American Economic Review*, Suppl. (March), pp. 139-165.

Costanza, R. (1980), 'Embodied Energy and Economic Valuation', *Science*, vol. 210, pp. 1219-1224.

Diamond, P.A. (1965), 'National Debt in a Neo-Classical Growth Model', *American Economic Review*, vol. 55 (5), pp. 1126-1150.

Domar, E.D. (1946), 'Capital Expansion, Rate of Growth and Employment', *Econometrica*, vol. 14 (April), pp. 137-147.

Domar, E.D. (1947), 'Expansion and Employment', *American Economic Review*, vol. 37 (1), pp. 343-355.

Domar, E.D. et al. (1964), 'Economic Growth and Productivity in the United States, Canada, United Kingdom, Germany and Japan in the Post-War Period', *Review Economic Statistics*, vol. 46 (1), pp. 33-40.

Durand, J.D. (1977), 'Historical Estimates of World Population: an Evaluation', *Population and Development Review*, vol. 3 (3), pp. 253-269.

Energy Statistics Yearbook 1993 (1995), UN, New York.

Ferguson, C.E. (1969), *The Neo-Classical Theory of Production and Distribution*, Cambridge University Press, Cambridge.

Gale, D. (1960), *The Theory of Linear Economic Models*, McGraw-Hill, Aucland *etc.*

Georgescu-Roegen, N. (1971), *The Entropy Law and the Economic Process*, Harvard University Press, Cambridge MA.

Gilland, B. (1995), 'World Population, Economic Growth, and Energy Demand, 1990-2100: A Review of Projections', *Population and Development Review*, vol. 21 (3), pp. 507-539.

Gramm, W.S. (1988), 'The Movement from Real to Abstract Value Theory, 1817-1959', *Cambridge Journal of Economics*, 1988, vol. 12 (2), pp. 225-246.

Griliches, Z. (1979), 'Issues in Assessing the Contribution of Research and Development to Productivity Growth', *Bell Journal of Economics*, vol. 10, pp. 92-116.

Griliches, Z. (1988), 'Productivity Puzzles and R & D: Another Nonexplanation', *Journal of Economics Perspectives*, vol. 2 (4), p. 9-21.

Gromov, G.P. (1985), *Natsionalnije informatsionnije resursi: problemi promishlennoi ekspluatatsii, in Russian (The National Information Resources: Problems of Industrial Exploitation)*, Nauka, Moscow.

Grossman, G.M. and Helpman, E. (1994), 'Endogenous Innovation in the Theory of Growth', *Journal of Economic Perspectives*, vol. 8 (1), pp. 23-44.

Hannon, B. and Joyce, J. (1981), 'Energy and Technical Progress', *Energy – The International Journal* vol. 6, pp. 187-195.

Harrod, R.F. (1939), 'An Essay in Dynamic Theory', *Economic Journal*, vol. 49 (March), pp. 14-23.

Harrod, R.F. (1948), *Towards a Dynamic Economics*, Macmillan, London.

Harrod, R.F. (1969), *Money*, Macmillan, London.

Hicks, J.R. (1946) *Value and Capital, 2nd Ed*, Clarendon Press, Oxford.

Historical Statistics of the United States: Colonial Times to 1970 (1975), Parts 1 & 2, US Department of Commerce, Washington.

Hudson, E.A. and Jorgenson, D.W. (1974), 'U.S. Energy Policy and Economic Growth, 1975-2000', *Bell Journal of Economics and Management Science*, vol. 5, pp. 461-514.

International Financial Statistics Yearbook (1997), International Monetary Fund.

Intriligator, M.D. (1971), *Mathematical Optimisation and Economic Theory*, Prentice-Hall, Englewood Cliffs NJ.

Kendrick, J. W., assisted by Y. Lethem and J. Rowley (1976), *The Formation and Stocks of Total Capital*, Columbia University Press for the National Bureau of Economic Research, New York.

Klenow, P.J. and Rodrigues-Clare A. (1997), 'Economic Growth: A Review Essay', *Journal of Monetary Economics*, vol. 40, pp. 597-617.

Kondratiev, N.D. (1989), *Problemi economicheskoi dinamiki, in Russian (Some Problems of Economic Dynamics)*, Economika, Moscow.

Korn, G.A. and Korn, T.M. (1968), *Mathematical Handbook for Scientists and Engineers*, McGraw-Hill, New York *etc.*

Kornai, J. (1975), *Anti-Equilibrium. On Economic Systems Theory and the Tasks of Research, 2nd Ed.*, North-Holland Publishing, Amsterdam and Oxford.

Kümmel, R. (1982), 'The Impact of Energy on Industrial Growth', *Energy – The International Journal*, vol. 7 (2), pp. 189-203.

Kümmel, R. (1989), 'Energy as a Factor of Production and Entropy as a Pollution Indicator in Macroeconomic Modelling', *Ecological Economics*, vol. 1 (1), 161-180.

Kümmel, R. and Lindenberger, D. (1999), 'The Productive Power of Energy and Economic Evolution', *Indian Journal of Applied Economics*, to be published.

Kümmel, R., Strassl, A., Goesner, A. and Eichhorn, W. (1985), 'Technical Progress and Energy Dependent Production Functions', *Zeitschrift für Nationaleokonomie*, vol. 45 (3), pp. 285-311.

Lancaster, K. (1968), *Mathematical Economics*, Macmillan, London.

Leontief, W.W. (1936), 'Quantitative Input and Output Relations in the Economic System of the United States', *Review of Economic Statistics*, vol. 18, pp. 105-125.

Leontief, W.W. (1941), *The Structure of the American Economy 1919–1939*, Harvard University Press, Cambridge MA.

Leontief, W.W. (1986), *Input-Output Economics, 2nd Ed.*, Oxford University Press, New York, Oxford.

Lotka, A.J. (1925), *Elements of Physical Biology*, Williams and Wilkins, Baltimore.

Lucas, R.E., Jr. (1988). 'On the Mechanics of Economic Development', *Journal of Monetary Economics*, vol. 22 (21), pp. 3-42.

McKenzie, L. (1959), 'On the Existence of General Equilibrium for a Competitive Market', *Econometrica*, vol. 27, pp. 54-71.

Maïsseu, A. and Voss, A. (1995), 'Energy, Entropy and Sustainable Development', *International Journal of Global Energy Issues*, vol. 8 (1-3), pp. 201-220.

Maltus, T.R. (1798), *An Essay on the Principles of Population, as it Affects the Future Improvement of Society*, J. Johnson, London.

Marshall, A. (1920), *Principle of Economics, 8th Edn*, Macmillan, London.

Marx, K. (1867), *Das Kapital. Kritik der Politischen Oekonomie*, Otto Meissner, Hamburg. English translation: Marx K. (1952), *Capital*, Encyclopaedia Britanica, Chicago *etc.*

Mirowski Ph. (1988), 'Energy and Energetics in Economic Theory: A Review Essay', *Journal of Economic Issues*, vol. 22 (4), pp. 811-830.

Morowitz, H.J. (1968), *Energy Flow in Biology. Biological Organisation as a Problem in Thermal Physics*, Academic Press, New York and London.

Mumford, L. (1934), *Technics and Civilisation*, Routledge and Kegan Paul, London.

Murray, J.D. (1989), *Mathematical Biology*, Springer-Verlag, Berlin *etc.*

Nakićenović, N., Gilli, P.V. and Kurz, R. (1996), 'Regional and Global Exergy and Energy Efficiencies', *Energy – The International Journal*, vol. 21 (3), pp. 223-237.

Narodnoje khozjaistvo SSSR in 1987 godu, in Russian (USSR Statistics Yearbook) (1988), Finansi i statistika, Moscow.

Newman, E.I. (1993), *Applied Ecology*, Blackwell Scientific Publications, London *etc.*

Nicolis, G. and Prigogine, I. (1977), *Self-Organisation in Non-Equilibrium Systems: From Dissipative Structures to Order through Fluctuations*, John Wiley and Sons, New York.

O'Connor, R. and Henry, E.W. (1975), *Input-Output Analysis and Its Applications*, Charles Griffin, London and High Wycomb.

Parikh, J.K. (1998), 'The Emperor Needs New Clothes: Long-Range Energy Use Scenarios by IIASA and IPCC', *Energy – The International Journal*, vol. 23 (9), pp. 69-70.

Pareto, V. (1909), *Manuel d'economie politique*, Girard et Briere, Paris.

Patterson, M.G. (1996), 'What is Energy Efficiency? Concepts, Indicators and Methodological Issues', *Energy Policy*, vol. 24 (5), pp. 377-390.

Pechurkin, N.S. (1982), *Energeticheskije aspekty nadorganizmennykh sistem, in Russian (Energy Aspects of Superorganism Systems)*, Nauka, Novosibirsk.

Polterovich, V.M. (1990), *Ekonomicheskoje ravnovesije i khozjaistvennyi mekanizm, in Russian (Equilibrium and Economical Mechanism)*, Nauka, Moscow.

Pokrovski, V.N. (1993), *Energija, teknnitsheskii progress i ekonomitsheskii rost. Prinzipi ekodinamiki, in Russian (Energy, Technical Progress and Economic Growth. Principles of Ecodynamics)*, Tradizija, Moscow.

Prigogine, I. (1980), *From Being to Becoming. Time and Complexity in the Physical Sciences*, Freeman & Company, New York.

Rakitskii, B. (1990), 'Towards the Revision of our Total Point of View on Distribution', *Voprosi economiki, in Russian*, No 11, pp. 3-13.

Ramsey, F.P. (1928), 'A Mathematical Theory of Saving', *Economic Journal*, vol. 38, pp. 543-559.

Reif, F. (1965), *Fundamentals of Statistical and Thermal Physics*, McGraw-Hill, Auckland *etc.*

Rivers, J.P.W. and Payne, P.R. (1982), 'The Comparison of Energy Supply and energy Needs: A Critique of Energy Requirements', in G.A. Harrison (ed), *Energy and Effort*, Taylor and Francis, London, pp. 85-105.

Romer, P.M. (1986), 'Increasing Returns and Long-Run Growth', *Journal of Political Economy*, vol. 94, pp. 1002-1037.

Romer, P.M. (1990), 'Endogenous Technological Change', *Journal of Political Economy*, vol. 98, pp. 71-102.

Samuelson, P.A. (1958), 'An Exact Consumption-Loan Model of Interest with or without the Social Contrivance of Money', *Journal of Political Economy* vol. 66 (6), pp. 467-482.

Samuelson, P. (1970), *Foundations of Economic Analysis*, Athenaeum, New York.

Say, J.B. (1803), *Tpaite d'economie politique on simple exposition de la maniere dont se forment, se distriduent, et se consomment les richesses*, t. 1-2, Deterville, Paris.

Schumpeter, J.A. (1911), *Theorie der wirtschaftlichen Entwicklung: Eine Untersuchung über Unternehmergewinn, Kapital, Kredit, Zins und den Kojunkturzyklus*, Dunker und Humblot, Berlin.

Schurr, S.H. and B.C. Netschert, B.C. (1960), *Energy in the American Economy, 1850-1975*, John Hopkius University Press, Baltimore MD.

Scott, M.FG. (1989), *A New View of Economic Growth*, Clarendon Press, Oxford.

Shapot, D.V., Belenkii V.Z. and Lukatskii A.M. (1995), 'Methods of Investigation of Economy-Energy Coupling', *Izvestija Akademii Nauk. Energetika, in Russian*, No 6, pp. 13-23.

Slutsky, E. (1915), 'Sulla teoria del bilancio del consumatore', *Giornale degli economisti*, vol. 60, pp. 19-23.

Smith, A. (1976), *An Inquiry into the Nature and Causes of the Wealth of Nations. In two volumes*, Vol. 1 and 2, Clarendon Press, Oxford.

Solow, R. (1957). 'Technical Change and the Aggregate Production Function', *Review of Economic Studies*, vol. 39 (Aug.), pp. 312-330.

Solow, R. (1970), *Growth Theory: An Exposition*, Clarendon Press, Oxford.

Solow, R. (1994), 'Perspective on Growth Theory', *Journal of Economic Perspectives*, vol. 8 (1), pp. 45-54.

Statistical Abstract of the United States 1980, 1986, 1989. (1980, 1986, 1989), US Department of Commerce, Washington.

Stephan, P.E. (1996), 'The Economics of Science', *Journal of Economic Literature*, vol.34 (3), pp. 1199-1235.

Verhulst, P.F. (1838), 'Notice sur la loi que la population suit dans son accroissement', *Corr. Math. et Phys.*, vol. 10, pp. 113 - 121.

Volterra, V. (1931), *Lesons sur la mathematique de la lutte pour la vie*, Marcel Brelot, Paris.

Von Neumann, J. (1937), 'Über ein okonomisches Gleichungssystem und eine Verallgemeinerung des Brouwerschen Fixpunktsatzes', *Ergebnisse eines Mathematischen Kolloqueiums*, vol. 8, pp. 73-83.

Von Neumann, J. and Morgenstern, O. (1953), *Theory of Games and Economic Behaviour, 3d Ed.*, Princeton University Press, Princeton.

Voslenskii, M.S. (1984), *Nomenklatura. The Soviet Ruling Class*, Doubleday.

Wald, A. (1951), 'On Some System of Equations of Mathematical Economics', *Econometrica*, vol. 19, pp. 368-403.

Walras, L. (1874), *Elements d'economie politique pure ou theorie de la richesse sociale*, Corbaz, Lausanne.

Wene, C.-O. (1996), 'Energy-Economy Analysis: Linking the Macroeconomic and Systems Engineering Approaches', *Energy – The International Journal*, vol. 21 (9), pp. 809-824.

White, L. (1949), *The Science of Culture*, Farrar, Straus, & Cudahy, New York.

World Population Projections, 1992 - 93 Edition (1992), John Hopkins University Press for the World Bank, Baltimore and London.

Zarnikau, J., Guermouche, S. and Schmidt, Ph. (1996), 'Can Different Energy Resources be Added or Compared?', *Energy – The International Journal*, vol. 21 (6), pp. 483-491.

Subject Index

DATE DUE

			Printed in USA

HIGHSMITH #45230